The Faber Book of Beasts

The Faber Book of
BEASTS

edited by Paul Muldoon

faber and faber

First published in 2010
by Faber and Faber Ltd
Bloomsbury House
74–77 Great Russell Street,
London, WC1B 3DA

This paperback edition first published in 1998
Photoset by Intype London Ltd
Printed and bound in the UK by
CPI Group (UK) Ltd, Croydon, CR0 4YY

A CIP record for this book
is available from the British Library

ISBN 978-0-571-19547-3

12 14 16 18 20 19 17 15 13 11

Contents

Introduction

It seems that in poetry, as in life, animals bring out the best in us. We are most human in the presence of animals, most humble, and it is only out of humility, out of uncertainty, out of ignorance, that the greatest art may be made.

The greatest anthologies, by contrast, are made by those, knowledgeable or otherwise, for whom uncertainty is a dirty word. Anthologists tend to be extremely arrogant, perhaps even despotic. The anthologist's introduction, meanwhile, is generally an attempt by a despot to account for his or her despotism, to present it as being both reasonable and benevolent. In that respect, my introduction will not disappoint.

Let me announce, then, that my purpose here is to present a selection of the best animal poems in the English-speaking tradition. Hardly are those words out when exceptions begin to slouch and slip and slither their way across the screen. These include a goodly number of translations of poems by such writers as Dante Alighieri, Amichai, Aristophanes, Arp, Baudelaire, Brodsky, Herbert, Holub, Homer, Horace, La Fontaine, Oppian, Ovid, Ponge, Sorescu and Virgil that have been taken over, to a greater or lesser extent, into the English tradition.

In general, though, I've decided to draw the line at poetry in translation, despite the fact that it will deprive many readers of much wonderful poetry from the Welsh, Scottish and Irish traditions, not to speak of the other traditions in which I myself have an interest, notably the Native American and Innuit, with their mesmerizing evocations of, or invocations to, the ptarmigan, the polar bear, the walrus and blubbery seal.

The very first animal poems (among the first poems of any kind) in most cultures must have been such hunting charms or spells, and something of their magical quality carries over into the earliest depictions of animals in poetry in English – the dragon in *Beowulf*, 'The Whale', the swan, cuckoo, barnacle goose, bull, bookworm and sea-suckled oyster of the *Exeter Book* riddles – right the way up to Francis Ponge's 'The Oyster' and Seamus Heaney's 'Oysters'.

Mention of these two poems, neither of which has made it to the final cut of this anthology, affords me the opportunity to say one or two things about the structure and method of the book. Firstly, I simply cannot include *all* of the best animal poems. To have made this book as doorstoppingly expansive as I'd have liked would have been to make it much more expensive than you'd have liked. My editor, Christopher Reid, was as properly insistent on the need to cull as he was to corral some farflung items (such as the extract from William Diaper's 'Oppian's *Halieuticks*') with which I myself was not familiar. I should make it clear, by the way, that a poem by Christopher Reid is roped in here at my insistence rather than his.

So, while some great poems may have slipped through the net, as it were, because I simply haven't come across them (this anthologist's arrogance is not quite total), many such as that Heaney, that Ponge, are missing simply because of the exigencies of space. Often, I've cut back on the number of poems by individual authors when it seemed that they figured too strongly in the book, so that the very brilliance of Heaney or Hughes or Moore or Lawrence or Frost or Dickinson began to weigh against them.

Not only do I feel a pang at having to let go of two such poems, I regret almost more the fact that those Heaney and Ponge oysters no longer sit prettily together, in provocative propinquity, as if on a bed of ice. The alphabetical method of the anthology allows for a great number of such felicitous fusions, so that a reader will move delightedly from Edward Thomas's 'Cock-Crow' to Henry Vaughan's 'Cock-Crowing', from Louis MacNeice's 'Elephants' to Marianne Moore's, from William Carlos Williams's 'The Horse' to Edwin Muir's 'The Horses', from Seamus Heaney's 'The Skunk' to a poem that influenced it, Robert Lowell's 'Skunk Hour'.

Such instances of poems being in dialogue with each other abound in this anthology. 'Skunk Hour' is linked, formally and thematically, to Elizabeth Bishop's 'Armadillo' ('Her son's a bishop.'), though it also nods in the direction of Marianne Moore (*'wedge*-head', '*ostrich* tail'). Thomas Hardy's 'The Fallow Deer at the Lonely House' winks at Edward Thomas's 'Out in the Dark', itself part-Hardy, part-Frost.

In a similar fashion, Frost's 'The Cow in Apple Time' draws on a technique of repetition similar to that used by John Clare in 'The Badger'. Richard Wilbur's 'The Ride' is a response to Frost's 'The Draft Horse' (itself a response to his own much-anthologized 'Stopping By Woods on a Snowy Evening'). In 'The Span of Life', Frost writes with an epigrammatic pithiness reminiscent of Pope:

> The old dog barks backwards without getting up.
> I can remember when he was a pup.

The speaker of Ted Hughes's 'Wodwo' (with his, or its, 'What am I?') barks right the way backwards to the riddling beasts of *The Exeter Book*.

This ongoing question of 'What am I?' is, indeed, central not only to animal poetry but to all forms of poetry. For if, as Wallace Stevens argues in his essay 'The Noble Rider and the Sound of Words', the function of the poet 'is to help people to live their lives', it might also be argued that nowhere is that responsibility thrown into sharper relief than in our accounts of the parallel lives of 'our little kinsmen'. For there, almost uniquely, do we see ourselves not only for who and what we are, but glimpse the possibility of what we might become. 'Near this spot,' as Byron wrote of his Newfoundland dog, Boatswain, 'are deposited the remains of one who possessed beauty without vanity, strength without insolence, courage without ferocity, and all the virtues of man without his vices.'

Abnegation

The red fox, the vixen
dancing in the half-light among the junipers,
wise-looking in a sexy way,
Egyptian-supple in her sharpness –
what does she want
with the dreams of dead vixens,
the apotheosis of Reynard,
the literature of fox-hunting?
Only in her nerves the past
sings, a thrill of self-preservation.
I go along down the road
to a house nailed together by Scottish
Covenanters, instinct mortified
in a virgin forest,
and she springs toward her den
every hair on her pelt alive
with tidings of the immaculate present.
They left me a westernness,
a birthright, a redstained, ravelled
afghan of sky.
She has no archives,
no heirlooms, no future
except death
and I could be more
her sister than theirs
who chopped their way across these hills
– a chosen people

ADRIENNE RICH

Address to the Beasts

For us who, from the moment
we first are worlded,
lapse into disarray,

who seldom know exactly
what we are up to,
and, as a rule, don't want to,

what a joy to know,
even when we can't see or hear you,
that you are around,

though very few of you
find us worth looking at,
unless we come too close.

To you all scents are sacred
except our smell and those
we manufacture.

How promptly and ably
you execute Nature's policies,
and are never

lured into misconduct
except by some unlucky
chance imprinting.

Endowed from birth with good manners,
you wag no snobbish elbows,
don't leer,

don't look down your nostrils,
nor poke them into another
creature's business.

Your own habitations
are cosy and private, not
pretentious temples.

Of course, you have to take lives
to keep your own, but never
kill for applause.

Compared with even your greediest,
how Non-U
our hunting gentry seem.

Exempt from taxation,

/ 2

you have never felt the need
to become literate,

but your oral cultures
have inspired our poets to pen
dulcet verses,

and, though unconscious of God,
your Sung Eucharists are
more hallowed than ours.

Instinct is commonly said
to rule you: I would call it
Common Sense.

If you cannot engender
a genius like Mozart,
neither can you

plague the earth
with brilliant sillies like Hegel
or clever nasties like Hobbes.

Shall we ever become adulted,
as you all soon do?
It seems unlikely.

Indeed, one balmy day,
we might well become,
not fossils, but vapour.

Distinct now,
in the end we shall join you
(how soon all corpses look alike),

but you exhibit no signs
of knowing that you are sentenced.
Now, could that be why

we upstarts are often
jealous of your innocence,
but never envious?

W. H. AUDEN

The Albatross

After Baudelaire, L'Albatros

Often, for a gag, the Jack Tars like to catch an albatross, Aviator
Of the high seas, who, following the navy, wants to be its Avatar.

But they slap him, Emperor of Blue, down on the salty planks. They
  taunt him.
Spat at, tripped up, his wings creak helplessly like oars, and haunt
  him.

This wingèd voyager, now bedraggled, ugly, awkward, how pathetic!
Someone pokes a pipe into his mouth, and someone else who mimics
  him is paralytic.

The Poet's like that Prince of Clouds, who soars above the archer and
  the hurricane: Great Auk
Brought down to earth, his gawky, gorgeous wings impede his walking.

CIARAN CARSON

Animal Acts

A bear who eats with a silver spoon.
Two apes adept at grave-digging.
Rats who do calculus.
A police dog who copulates with a woman,
Who takes undertaker's measurements.

A bedbug who suffers, who has doubts
About his existence. The miraculous
Laughing dove. A thousand-year-old turtle
Playing billiards. A chicken who
Cuts his own throat, who bleeds.

The trainer with his sugar-cubes,
With his chair and whip. The evenings

/ 4

When they all huddle in a cage,
Smoking cheap cigars, lazily
Marking the cards in the new deck.

CHARLES SIMIC

Apartment Cats

The Girls wake, stretch, and pad up to the door.
    They rub my leg and purr:
    One sniffs around my shoe,
    Rich with an outside smell,
  The other rolls back on the floor –
White bib exposed, and stomach of soft fur.

Now, more awake, they re-enact Ben Hur
    Along the corridor,
    Wheel, gallop; as they do,
    Their noses twitching still,
  Their eyes get wild, their bodies tense,
Their usual prudence seemingly withdraws.

And then they wrestle: parry, lock of paws,
    Blind hug of close defence,
    Tail-thump, and smothered mew.
    If either, though, feels claws,
  She abruptly rises, knowing well
How to stalk off in wise indifference.

THOM GUNN

An Appeal to Cats in the Business of Love

Ye cats that at midnight spit love at each other,
Who best feel the pangs of a passionate lover,
I appeal to your scratches and your tattered fur,
If the business of Love be no more than to purr.

Old Lady Grimalkin with her gooseberry eyes,
Knew something when a kitten, for why she is wise;
You find by experience, the love-fit's soon o'er,
Puss! Puss! lasts not long, but turns to *Cat-whore!*
 Men ride many miles,
 Cats tread many tiles,
 Both hazard their necks in the fray;
 Only cats, when they fall
 From a house or a wall,
 Keep their feet, mount their tails, and away!

THOMAS FLATMAN

from Arcadia

The multitude to *Ioue* a sute imparts,
 With neighing, blaying, braying, and barking,
 Roring and howling, for to haue a king.
A king in language theirs they said they would,
(For then their language was a perfect speech)
The Byrds likewise which chirpes and puing could,
Cackling and chattering, that of *Ioue* beseech,
Only the Owle still warnd them not to seech,
 So hastily, that, which they would repent;
 But saw they would, and he to desarts went.
Ioue wisely said (for wisedome wisely saies)
O Beasts take heed what you of me desire,
Rulers will thinke all things made them to please,
And soone forget the swinke due to their hire,
But since you will part of my heauenly fire,
 I will you lend, the rest your selues must giue,
 That it both seene and felt may with you liue.
Full glad they were, and tooke the naked sprite
Which strait the earth ycloathed in his clay:
The Lyon hart: the Ownce gaue actiue might.
The Horse good shape; the Sparrow lust to play,
Nightingale voyce, entising songs to say.
 Elephant gaue a perfect memory,

And Parrot ready toong that to apply.
The Foxe gaue craft; the Dogge gaue flattery,
Asse patience; the Mole a working thought:
Eagle high thought, Wolfe secret crueltie,
Monky sweet breath; the Cow her faire eyes brought
The Ermion whitest skin, spotted with nought.

The Sheepe mild seeming face, climing the Beare,
The Stag did giue the harme-eschuing feare.
The Hare her sleights, the Cat his melancholy,
Ant industry, and Conny skill to build:
Cranes order; Storkes to be appearing holy.
Camelion ease to chaunge, Ducke ease to yeeld,
Crocodile teares, which might be falsly spild.

Ape greeting gaue, though he did mowing stand,
The instrument of instruments the hand.

PHILIP SIDNEY

Ariel

Stasis in darkness.
Then the substanceless blue
Pour of tor and distances.

God's lioness,
How one we grow,
Pivot of heels and knees! – The furrow

Splits and passes, sister to
The brown arc
Of the neck I cannot catch,

Nigger-eye
Berries cast dark
Hooks –

Black sweet blood mouthfuls,
Shadows.
Something else

Hauls me through air –
Thighs, hair;
Flakes from my heels.

White
Godiva, I unpeel –
Dead hands, dead stringencies.

And now I
Foam to wheat, a glitter of seas.
The child's cry

Melts in the wall.
And I
Am the arrow,

The dew that flies
Suicidal, at one with the drive
Into the red

Eye, the cauldron of morning.

SYLVIA PLATH

The Armadillo

For Robert Lowell

This is the time of year
when almost every night
the frail, illegal fire balloons appear.
Climbing the mountain height,

rising toward a saint
still honored in these parts,
the paper chambers flush and fill with light
that comes and goes, like hearts.

Once up against the sky it's hard
to tell them from the stars –
planets, that is – the tinted ones:
Venus going down, or Mars,

or the pale green one. With a wind,
they flare and falter, wobble and toss;
but if it's still they steer between
the kite sticks of the Southern Cross,

receding, dwindling, solemnly
and steadily forsaking us,
or, in the downdraft from a peak,
suddenly turning dangerous.

Last night another big one fell.
It splattered like an egg of fire
against the cliff behind the house.
The flame ran down. We saw the pair

of owls who nest there flying up
and up, their whirling black-and-white
stained bright pink underneath, until
they shrieked up out of sight.

The ancient owls' nest must have burned.
Hastily, all alone,
a glistening armadillo left the scene,
rose-flecked, head down, tail down,

and then a baby rabbit jumped out,
short-eared, to our surprise.
So soft! – a handful of intangible ash
with fixed, ignited eyes.

Too pretty, dreamlike mimicry!
O falling fire and piercing cry
and panic, and a weak mailed fist
clenched ignorant against the sky!

ELIZABETH BISHOP

As the Team's Head-Brass

As the team's head-brass flashed out on the turn
The lovers disappeared into the wood.
I sat among the boughs of the fallen elm
That strewed an angle of the fallow, and
Watched the plough narrowing a yellow square
Of charlock. Every time the horses turned
Instead of treading me down, the ploughman leaned
Upon the handles to say or ask a word,
About the weather, next about the war.
Scraping the share he faced towards the wood,
And screwed along the furrow till the brass flashed
Once more.
          The blizzard felled the elm whose crest
I sat in, by a woodpecker's round hole,
The ploughman said. 'When will they take it away?'
'When the war's over.' So the talk began –
One minute and an interval of ten,
A minute more and the same interval.
'Have you been out?' 'No.' 'And don't want to, perhaps?'
'If I could only come back again, I should.
I could spare an arm. I shouldn't want to lose
A leg. If I should lose my head, why, so,
I should want nothing more. . . . Have many gone
From here?' 'Yes.' 'Many lost?' 'Yes, a good few.
Only two teams work on the farm this year.
One of my mates is dead. The second day
In France they killed him. It was back in March,
The very night of the blizzard, too. Now if
He had stayed here we should have moved the tree.'
'And I should not have sat here. Everything
Would have been different. For it would have been
Another world.' 'Ay, and a better, though
If we could see all all might seem good.' Then
The lovers came out of the wood again:

The horses started and for the last time
I watched the clods crumble and topple over
After the ploughshare and the stumbling team.

EDWARD THOMAS

from Astrophel and Stella

I on my horse, and Love on me, doth try
   Our horsemanships, while by strange work I prove
   A horseman to my horse, a horse to Love,
And now man's wrongs in me, poor beast, descry.
The reins wherewith my rider doth me tie
   Are humbled thoughts, which bit of reverence move,
   Curb'd in with fear, but with gilt boss above
Of hope, which makes it seem fair to the eye.
   The wand is will; thou, fancy, saddle art,
Girt fast by memory; and while I spur
My horse, he spurs with sharp desire my heart.
He sits me fast, however I do stir,
   And now hath made me to his hand so right
   That in the manage myself take delight.

PHILIP SIDNEY

At Grass

The eye can hardly pick them out
From the cold shade they shelter in,
Till wind distresses tail and mane;
Then one crops grass, and moves about
– The other seeming to look on –
And stands anonymous again.

Yet fifteen years ago, perhaps
Two dozen distances sufficed
To fable them: faint afternoons

Of Cups and Stakes and Handicaps,
Whereby their names were artificed
To inlay faded, classic Junes –

Silks at the start: against the sky
Numbers and parasols: outside,
Squadrons of empty cars, and heat,
And littered grass: then the long cry
Hanging unhushed till it subside
To stop-press columns on the street.

Do memories plague their ears like flies?
They shake their heads. Dusk brims the shadows.
Summer by summer all stole away,
The starting-gates, the crowds and cries –
All but the unmolesting meadows.
Almanacked, their names live; they

Have slipped their names, and stand at ease,
Or gallop for what must be joy,
And not a fieldglass sees them home,
Or curious stop-watch prophesies:
Only the groom, and the groom's boy,
With bridles in the evening come.

    PHILIP LARKIN

At Woodward's Gardens

A boy, presuming on his intellect,
Once showed two little monkeys in a cage
A burning-glass they could not understand
And never could be made to understand.
Words are no good: to say it was a lens
For gathering solar rays would not have helped.
But let him show them how the weapon worked.
He made the sun a pinpoint on the nose
Of first one, then the other, till it brought
A look of puzzled dimness to their eyes
That blinking could not seem to blink away.

They stood arms laced together at the bars,
And exchanged troubled glances over life.
One put a thoughtful hand up to his nose
As if reminded – or as if perhaps
Within a million years of an idea.
He got his purple little knuckles stung.
The already known had once more been confirmed
By psychological experiment,
And that were all the finding to announce
Had the boy not presumed too close and long.
There was a sudden flash of arm, a snatch,
And the glass was the monkeys', not the boy's.
Precipitately they retired back-cage
And instituted an investigation
On their part, though without the needed insight.
They bit the glass and listened for the flavor.
They broke the handle and the binding off it.
Then none the wiser, frankly gave it up,
And having hid it in their bedding straw
Against the day of prisoners' ennui,
Came dryly forward to the bars again
To answer for themselves: Who said it mattered
What monkeys did or didn't understand?
They might not understand a burning-glass.
They might not understand the sun itself.
It's knowing what to do with things that counts.

ROBERT FROST

Auguries of Innocence

To see a World in a Grain of Sand
And a Heaven in a Wild Flower,
Hold Infinity in the palm of your hand
And Eternity in an hour.

A Robin Red breast in a Cage
Puts all Heaven in a Rage,

A dove house fill'd with doves & Pigeons
Shudders Hell thro' all its regions.
A dog starv'd at his Master's Gate
Predicts the ruin of the State.
A Horse misus'd upon the Road
Calls to Heaven for Human blood.
Each outcry of the hunted Hare
A fibre from the Brain does tear.
A Skylark wounded in the wing,
A Cherubim does cease to sing.
The Game Cock clip'd & arm'd for fight
Does the Rising Sun affright.
Every Wolf's & Lion's howl
Raises from Hell a Human Soul.
The wild deer, wand'ring here & there,
Keeps the Human Soul from Care.
The Lamb misus'd breeds Public strife
And yet forgives the Butcher's Knife.
The Bat that flits at close of Eve
Has left the Brain that won't Believe.
The Owl that calls upon the Night
Speaks the Unbeliever's fright.
He who shall hurt the little Wren
Shall never be belov'd by Men.
He who the Ox to wrath has mov'd
Shall never be by Woman lov'd.
The wanton Boy that kills the Fly
Shall feel the Spider's enmity.
He who torments the Chafer's sprite
Weaves a Bower in endless Night.
The Catterpiller on the Leaf
Repeats to thee thy Mother's grief.
Kill not the Moth nor Butterfly,
For the Last Judgment draweth nigh.
He who shall train the Horse to War
Shall never pass the Polar Bar.
The Beggar's Dog & Widow's Cat
Feed them & thou wilt grow fat.
The Gnat that sings his Summer's song
Poison gets from Slander's tongue.

/ 14

The poison of the Snake & Newt
Is the sweat of Envy's Foot.
The Poison of the Honey Bee
Is the Artist's Jealousy.
The Prince's Robes & Beggar's Rags
Are Toadstools on the Miser's Bags.
A truth that's told with bad intent
Beats all the Lies you can invent.
It is right it should be so;
Man was made for Joy & Woe;
And when this we rightly know
Thro' the World we safely go.
Joy & Woe are woven fine,
A Clothing for the Soul divine;
Under every grief & pine
Runs a joy with silken twine.
The Babe is more than swadling Bands;
Throughout all these Human Lands
Tools were made, & Born were hands,
Every Farmer Understands.
Every Tear from Every Eye
Becomes a Babe in Eternity;
This is caught by Females bright
And return'd to its own delight.
The Bleat, the Bark, Bellow & Roar
Are Waves that Beat on Heaven's Shore.
The Babe that weeps the Rod beneath
Writes Revenge in realms of death.
The Beggar's Rags, fluttering in Air,
Does to Rags the Heaven tear.
The Soldier, arm'd with Sword & Gun,
Palsied strikes the Summer's Sun.
The poor Man's Farthing is worth more
Than all the Gold on Afric's Shore.
One Mite wrung from the Labrer's hands
Shall buy & sell the Miser's Lands:
Or, if protected from on high,
Does that whole Nation sell & buy.
He who mocks the Infant's Faith
Shall be mock'd in Age & Death.

He who shall teach the Child to Doubt
The rotting Grave shall ne'er get out.
He who respects the Infant's faith
Triumphs over Hell & Death.
The Child's Toys & the Old Man's Reasons
Are the Fruits of the Two seasons.
The Questioner, who sits so sly,
Shall never know how to Reply.
He who replies to words of Doubt
Doth put the Light of Knowledge out.
The Strongest Poison ever known
Came from Caesar's Laurel Crown.
Nought can deform the Human Race
Like to the Armour's iron brace.
When Gold & Gems adorn the Plow
To peaceful Arts shall Envy Bow.
A Riddle or the Cricket's Cry
Is to Doubt a fit Reply.
The Emmet's Inch & Eagle's Mile
Make Lame Philosophy to smile.
He who Doubts from what he sees
Will ne'er Believe, do what you Please.
If the Sun & Moon should doubt,
They'd immediately Go out.
To be in a Passion you Good may do,
But no Good if a Passion is in you.
The Whore & Gambler, by the State
Licenc'd, build that Nation's Fate.
The Harlot's cry from Street to Street
Shall weave Old England's winding Sheet.
The Winner's Shout, the Loser's Curse,
Dance before dead England's Hearse.
Every Night & every Morn
Some to Misery are Born.
Every Morn & every Night
Some are Born to sweet delight.
Some are Born to sweet delight,
Some are Born to Endless Night.
We are led to Believe a Lie
When we see not Thro' the Eye

Which was Born in a Night to perish in a Night
When the Soul Slept in Beams of Light.
God Appears & God is Light
To those poor Souls who dwell in Night,
But does a Human Form Display
To those who Dwell in Realms of day.

WILLIAM BLAKE

Baa Baa Black Sheep

Baa, baa, black sheep,
  Have you any wool?
Yes, sir, yes, sir,
  Three bags full;
One for the master,
  And one for the dame,
And one for the little boy
  Who lives down the lane.

ANONYMOUS

Baby Tortoise

You know what it is to be born alone,
Baby tortoise!

The first day to heave your feet little by little from the shell,
Not yet awake,
And remain lapsed on earth,
Not quite alive.

A tiny, fragile, half-animate bean.

To open your tiny beak-mouth, that looks as if it would never open,
Like some iron door;
To lift the upper hawk-beak from the lower base
And reach your skinny little neck

And take your first bite at some dim bit of herbage,
Alone, small insect,
Tiny bright-eye,
Slow one.

To take your first solitary bite
And move on your slow, solitary hunt.
Your bright, dark little eye,
Your eye of a dark disturbed night,
Under its slow lid, tiny baby tortoise,
So indomitable.

No one ever heard you complain.

You draw your head forward, slowly, from your little wimple
And set forward, slow-dragging, on your four-pinned toes,
Rowing slowly forward.
Whither away, small bird?

Rather like a baby working its limbs,
Except that you make slow, ageless progress
And a baby makes none.

The touch of sun excites you,
And the long ages, and the lingering chill
Make you pause to yawn,
Opening your impervious mouth,
Suddenly beak-shaped, and very wide, like some suddenly gaping
    pincers;
Soft red tongue, and hard thin gums,
Then close the wedge of your little mountain front,
Your face, baby tortoise.

Do you wonder at the world, as slowly you turn your head in its
    wimple
And look with laconic, black eyes?
Or is sleep coming over you again,
The non-life?

You are so hard to wake.

Are you able to wonder?
Or is it just your indomitable will and pride of the first life
Looking round

And slowly pitching itself against the inertia
Which had seemed invincible?

The vast inanimate,
And the fine brilliance of your so tiny eye,
Challenger.

Nay, tiny shell-bird,
What a huge vast inanimate it is, that you must row against,
What an incalculable inertia.

Challenger,
Little Ulysses, fore-runner,
No bigger than my thumb-nail,
Buon viaggio.

All animate creation on your shoulder,
Set forth, little Titan, under your battle-shield.

The ponderous, preponderate,
Inanimate universe;
And you are slowly moving, pioneer, you alone.

How vivid your travelling seems now, in the troubled sunshine,
Stoic, Ulyssean atom;
Suddenly hasty, reckless, on high toes.

Voiceless little bird,
Resting your head half out of your wimple
In the slow dignity of your eternal pause.
Alone, with no sense of being alone,
And hence six times more solitary;
Fulfilled of the slow passion of pitching through immemorial ages
Your little round house in the midst of chaos.

Over the garden earth,
Small bird,
Over the edge of all things.

Traveller,

With your tail tucked a little on one side
Like a gentleman in a long-skirted coat.

All life carried on your shoulder,
Invincible fore-runner.

D. H. LAWRENCE

The Badger

The badger grunting on his woodland track
With shaggy hide and sharp nose scrowed with black
Roots in the bushes and the woods and makes
A great hugh burrow in the ferns and brakes
With nose on ground he runs a awkard pace
And anything will beat him in the race
The shepherds dog will run him to his den
Followed and hooted by the dogs and men
The woodman when the hunting comes about
Go round at night to stop the foxes out
And hurrying through the bushes ferns and brakes
Nor sees the many holes the badger makes
And often through the bushes to the chin
Breaks the old holes and tumbles headlong in

When midnight comes a host of dogs and men
Go out and track the badger to his den
And put a sack within the hole and lye
Till the old grunting badger passes bye
He comes and hears they let the strongest loose
The old fox hears the noise and drops the goose
The poacher shoots and hurrys from the cry
And the old hare half wounded buzzes bye
They get a forked stick to bear him down
And clapt the dogs and bore him to the town
And bait him all the day with many dogs
And laugh and shout and fright the scampering hogs
He runs along and bites at all he meets
They shout and hollo down the noisey streets

He turns about to face the loud uproar
And drives the rebels to their very doors
The frequent stone is hurled where ere they go
When badgers fight and every ones a foe
The dogs are clapt and urged to join the fray
The badger turns and drives them all away
Though scarcely half as big dimute and small
He fights with dogs for hours and beats them all
The heavy mastiff savage in the fray
Lies down and licks his feet and turns away
The bull dog knows his match and waxes cold
The badger grins and never leaves his hold
He drives the crowd and follows at their heels
And bites them through the drunkard swears and reels

The frighted women takes the boys away
The blackguard laughs and hurrys on the fray
He trys to reach the woods a awkard race
But sticks and cudgels quickly stop the chace
He turns agen and drives the noisey crowd
And beats the many dogs in noises loud
He drives away and beats them every one
And then they loose them all and set them on
He falls as dead and kicked by boys and men
Then starts and grins and drives the crowd agen
Till kicked and torn and beaten out he lies
And leaves his hold and cackles groans and dies

Some keep a baited badger tame as hog
And tame him till he follows like the dog
They urge him on like dogs and show fair play
He beats and scarcely wounded goes away
Lapt up as if asleep he scorns to fly
And siezes any dog that ventures nigh
Clapt like a dog he never bites the men
But worrys dogs and hurrys to his den
They let him out and turn a barrow down
And there he fights the pack of all the town
He licks the patting hand and trys to play

And never trys to bite or run away
And runs away from noise in hollow trees
Burnt by the boys to get a swarm of bees

JOHN CLARE

Bat

At evening, sitting on this terrace,
When the sun from the west, beyond Pisa, beyond the mountains of
  Carrara
Departs, and the world is taken by surprise . . .

When the tired flower of Florence is in gloom beneath the glowing
Brown hills surrounding . . .

When under the arches of the Ponte Vecchio
A green light enters against stream, flush from the west,
Against the current of obscure Arno . . .

Look up, and you see things flying
Between the day and the night;
Swallows with spools of dark thread sewing the shadows together.

A circle swoop, and a quick parabola under the bridge arches
Where light pushes through;
A sudden turning upon itself of a thing in the air.
A dip to the water.

And you think:
'The swallows are flying so late!'

Swallows?

Dark air-life looping
Yet missing the pure loop . . .
A twitch, a twitter, an elastic shudder in flight
And serrated wings against the sky,
Like a glove, a black glove thrown up at the light,
And falling back.

Never swallows!
Bats!
The swallows are gone.

At a wavering instant the swallows give way to bats
By the Ponte Vecchio . . .
Changing guard.

Bats, and an uneasy creeping in one's scalp
As the bats swoop overhead!
Flying madly.

Pipistrello!
Black piper on an infinitesimal pipe.
Little lumps that fly in air and have voices indefinite, wildly vindictive;

Wings like bits of umbrella.

Bats!
Creatures that hang themselves up like an old rag, to sleep;
And disgustingly upside down.
Hanging upside down like rows of disgusting old rags
And grinning in their sleep.
Bats!

In China the bat is symbol of happiness.

Not for me!

D. H. LAWRENCE

The Bear

The bear puts both arms around the tree above her
And draws it down as if it were a lover
And its chokecherries lips to kiss good-by,
Then lets it snap back upright in the sky.
Her next step rocks a boulder on the wall
(She's making her cross-country in the fall).
Her great weight creaks the barbed wire in its staples
As she flings over and off down through the maples,

Leaving on one wire tooth a lock of hair.
Such is the uncaged progress of the bear.
The world has room to make a bear feel free;
The universe seems cramped to you and me.
Man acts more like the poor bear in a cage,
That all day fights a nervous inward rage,
His mood rejecting all his mind suggests.
He paces back and forth and never rests
The toenail click and shuffle of his feet,
The telescope at one end of his beat,
And at the other end the microscope,
Two instruments of nearly equal hope,
And in conjunction giving quite a spread.
Or if he rests from scientific tread,
'Tis only to sit back and sway his head
Through ninety-odd degrees of arc, it seems,
Between two metaphysical extremes.
He sits back on his fundamental butt
With lifted snout and eyes (if any) shut
(He almost looks religious but he's not),
And back and forth he sways from cheek to cheek,
At one extreme agreeing with one Greek,
At the other agreeing with another Greek,
Which may be thought, but only so to speak.
A baggy figure, equally pathetic
When sedentary and when peripatetic.

ROBERT FROST

The Beasts' Confession to the Priest

When beasts could speak, (the learned say
They still can do so every day)
It seems, they had religion then,
As much as now we find in men.
It happened when a plague broke out,
(Which therefore made them more devout)
The king of brutes (to make it plain,

Of quadrupeds I only mean)
By proclamation gave command,
That every subject in the land
Should to the priest confess their sins;
And, thus the pious wolf begins:

'Good father, I must own with shame,
That, often I have been to blame:
I must confess, on Friday last,
Wretch that I was, I broke my fast:
But, I defy the basest tongue
To prove I did my neighbour wrong;
Or ever went to seek my food
By rapine, theft, or thirst of blood.'

The ass approaching next, confessed,
That in his heart he loved a jest:
A wag he was, he needs must own,
And could not let a dunce alone:
Sometimes his friend he would not spare,
And might perhaps be too severe:
But yet, the worst that could be said,
He was a *wit* both born and bred;
And if it be a sin or shame,
Nature alone must bear the blame:
One fault he hath, is sorry for't,
His ears are half a foot too short;
Which could he to the standard bring,
He'd show his face before the king:
Then, for his voice, there's none disputes
That he's the nightingale of brutes.

The swine with contrite heart allowed,
His shape and beauty made him proud:
In diet was perhaps too nice,
But gluttony was ne'er his vice:
In every turn of life content,
And meekly took what fortune sent:
Inquire through all the parish round
A better neighbour ne'er was found:
His vigilance might some displease;

'Tis true, he hated sloth like pease.

The mimic ape began his chatter,
How evil tongues his life bespatter:
Much of the censuring world complained,
Who said, his gravity was feigned:
Indeed, the strictness of his morals
Engaged him in a hundred quarrels:
He saw, and he was grieved to see't,
His zeal was sometimes indiscreet:
He found, his virtues too severe
For our corrupted times to bear;
Yet, such a lewd licentious age
Might well excuse a stoic's rage.

The goat advanced with decent pace;
And, first excused his youthful face;
Forgiveness begged, that he appeared
('Twas nature's fault) without a beard.
'Tis true, he was not much inclined
To fondness for the female kind;
Not, as his enemies object,
From chance, or natural defect;
Not by a frigid constitution;
But, through a pious resolution;
For, he had made a holy vow
Of chastity, as monks do now;
Which he resolved to keep for ever hence,
As strictly too, as doth his reverence.

Apply the tale, and you shall find
How just it suits with humankind.
Some faults we own: but, can you guess?
Why! – virtues carried to excess;
Wherewith our vanity endows us,
Though neither foe nor friend allows us.

The lawyer swears, you may rely on't,
He never squeezed a needy client:
And, this he makes his constant rule;
For which his brethren call him fool:
His conscience always was so nice,

He freely gave the poor advice;
By which he lost, he may affirm,
A hundred fees last Easter term.
While others of the learned robe
Would break the patience of a Job,
No pleader at the bar could match
His diligence and quick dispatch;
Ne'er kept a cause, he well may boast,
Above a term or two at most.

The cringing knave who seeks a place
Without success; thus tells his case:
Why should he longer mince the matter?
He failed, because he could not flatter:
He had not learnt to turn his coat,
Nor for a party give his vote:
His crime he quickly understood;
Too zealous for the nation's good:
He found, the ministers resent it,
Yet could not in his heart repent it.

The chaplain vows, he cannot fawn,
Though it would raise him to the lawn:
He passed his hours among his books;
You find it in his meagre looks:
He might, if he were worldly-wise,
Preferment get, and spare his eyes:
But owned, he had a stubborn spirit
That made him trust alone in merit:
Would rise by merit to promotion;
Alas! a mere chimeric notion.

The doctor, if you will believe him,
Confessed a sin, and God forgive him:
Called up at midnight, ran to save
A blind old beggar from the grave:
But, see how Satan spreads his snares;
He quite forgot to say his prayers.
He cannot help it for his heart
Sometimes to act the parson's part:
Quotes from the bible many a sentence

That moves his patients to repentance:
And, when his medicines do no good,
Supports their mind with heavenly food.
At which, however well intended,
He hears the clergy are offended;
And grown so bold behind his back
To call him hypocrite and quack.
In his own church he keeps a seat;
Says grace before, and after meat;
And calls, without affecting airs,
His household twice a day to prayers.
He shuns apothecary's shops;
And hates to cram the sick with slops;
He scorns to make his art a trade;
Nor bribes my Lady's favourite maid.
Old nurse-keepers would never hire
To recommend him to the squire;
Which others, whom he will not name,
Have often practised to their shame.

 The statesman tells you with a sneer,
His fault is to be too sincere;
And, having no siníster ends,
Is apt to disoblige his friends.
The nation's good, his master's glory,
Without regard to Whig or Tory,
Were all the schemes he had in view;
Yet he was seconded by few:
Though some had spread a thousand lies;
'Twas *he* defeated the Excise.
'Twas known, though he had borne aspersion;
That, standing troops were his aversion:
His practice was, in every station
To serve the king, and please the nation.
Though hard to find in every case
The fittest man to fill a place:
His promises he ne'er forgot,
But took memorials on the spot:
His enemies, for want of charity,
Said, he affected popularity:

'Tis true, the people understood,
That all he did was for their good;
Their kind affections he has tried;
No love is lost on either side.
He came to court with fortune clear,
Which now he runs out every year;
Must, at the rate that he goes on,
Inevitably be undone.
Oh! if his Majesty would please
To give him but a writ of ease,
Would grant him licence to retire,
As it hath long been his desire,
By fair accounts it would be found
He's poorer by ten thousand pound.
He owns, and hopes it is no sin,
He ne'er was partial to his kin;
He thought it base for men in stations,
To crowd the court with their relations;
His country was his dearest mother,
And every virtuous man his brother:
Through modesty, or awkward shame,
(For which he owns himself to blame)
He found the wisest men he could,
Without respect to friends, or blood,
Nor ever acts on private views,
When he hath liberty to choose.

　　The sharper swore he hated play,
Except to pass an hour away:
And, well he might; for, to his cost,
By want of skill, he always lost:
He heard, there was a club of cheats
Who had contrived a thousand feats;
Could change the stock, or cog a die,
And thus deceive the sharpest eye:
No wonder how his fortune sunk,
His brothers fleece him when he's drunk.

　　I own, the moral not exact;
Besides, the tale is false in fact;
And, so absurd, that I could raise up

From fields Elysian, fabling Aesop;
I would accuse him to his face
For libelling the four-foot race.
Creatures of every kind but ours
Well comprehend their natural powers;
While we, whom reason ought to sway,
Mistake our talents every day:
The ass was never known so stupid
To act the part of Tray, or Cupid;
Nor leaps upon his master's lap,
There to be stroked and fed with pap;
As Aesop would the world persuade;
He better understands his trade:
Nor comes whene'er his lady whistles;
But, carries loads, and feeds on thistles;
Our author's meaning, I presume, is
A creature *bipes et implumis*;
Wherein the moralist designed
A compliment to humankind:
For, here he owns, that now and then
Beasts may *degenerate* into men.

JONATHAN SWIFT

from The Beggar's Opera

Before the barn-door crowing,
  The Cock by Hens attended,
His eyes around him throwing,
  Stands for a while suspended:

Then one he singles from the crew,
  And cheers the happy Hen;
With how do you do, and how do you do,
  And how do you do again.

JOHN GAY

from Beowulf

The strong champion stood up beside his shield,
brave beneath helmet, he bore his mail-shirt
to the rocky cliff's foot, confident in his strength,
a single man; such is not the coward's way!
Then did the survivor of a score of conflicts,
the battle-clashes of encountering armies,
excelling in manhood, see in the wall
a stone archway, and out of the barrow broke
a stream surging through it, a stream of fire
with waves of deadly flame; the dragon's breath
meant he could not venture into the vault near the hoard
for any time at all without being burnt.

Passion filled the prince of the Geats:
be allowed a cry to utter from his breast,
roared from his stout heart: as the horn clear in battle
his voice re-echoed through the vault of grey stone.
The hoard-guard recognized a human voice,
and there was no more time for talk of friendship:
hatred stirred. Straightaway
the breath of the dragon billowed from the rock
in a hissing gust; the ground boomed.

He swung up his shield, overshadowed by the mound,
the lord of the Geats against this grisly stranger.
The temper of the twisted tangle-thing was fired
to close now in battle. The brave warrior-king
shook out his sword so sharp of edge,
an ancient heirloom. Each of the pair,
intending destruction, felt terror at the other:
intransigent beside his towering shield
the lord of friends, while the fleetness of the serpent
wound itself together; he waited in his armour.
It came flowing forward, flaming and coiling,
rushing on its fate.
                        For the famous prince
the protection lent to his life and person
by the shield was shorter than he had shaped it to be.

He must now dispute this space of time,
the first in his life when fate had not assigned him
the glory of the battle. The Geat chieftain
raised his hand, and reached down such a stroke
with his huge ancestral sword on the horribly-patterned snake
that, meeting the bone, its bright edge turned
and it bit less strongly than its sorely-straitened lord
required of it then. The keeper of the barrow
after this stroke grew savage in mood,
spat death-fire; the sparks of their battle
blazed into the distance.

       He boasted of no triumphs then,
the gold-friend of the Geats, for his good old sword
bared in the battle, his blade, had failed him,
as such iron should not do.

       That was no easy adventure,
when the celebrated son of Edgetheow
had to pass from that place on earth
and against his will take up his dwelling
in another place; as every man must give up
the days that are lent him.

       It was not long again
to the next meeting of those merciless ones.
The barrow-guard took heart; his breast heaved
with fresh out-breath: fire enclosed
the former folk-king; he felt bitter pain.

The band of picked companions did not come
to stand about him, as battle-usage asks,
offspring of athelings; they escaped to the wood,
saved their lives.

     Sorrow filled
the breast of one man. The bonds of kinship
nothing may remove for a man who thinks rightly.
This was *Wiglaf*, Weoxstan's son,
well-loved shieldsman, a Scylfing prince
of the stock of Alfhere; he could see his lord
tormented by the heat through his mask of battle.
He remembered then the favours he had formerly bestowed on him,
the wealthy dwelling-place of the Waymundings,

confirming him in the landrights his father had held.
He could not then hold back: hand gripped the yellow
linden-wood shield, shook out that ancient
sword that Eanmund, Ohthere's son,
had left among men.

                He met his end in battle,
a friendless exile, felled by the sword
wielded by Weoxstan: who went back to his kinsmen
with the shining helm, the shirt of ring-mail
and the ancient giant-sword. All this war-harness,
eager for use, Onela then gave to him,
though it had been his nephew's; nor did he speak
of the blood-feud to the killer of his brother's son.
Weoxstan kept this war-gear many years,
sword and breast-armour, till his son was able
to perform manly deeds as his father had of old.
He gave him among the Geats these garments of battle
of incalculable worth; then went his life's journey
wise and full of years.

                For the youthful warrior
this was the first occasion when he was called on to stand
at his dear lord's shoulder in the shock of battle.
His courage did not crumble, nor did his kinsman's heirloom
weaken at the war-play: as the worm found out
when they had got to grips with one another.

Wiglaf then spoke many words that were fitting,
addressed his companions; dark was his mood.
'I remember the time, as we were taking mead
in the banqueting hall, when we bound ourselves
to the gracious lord who granted us arms,
that we would make return for these trappings of war,
these helms and hard swords, if an hour such as this
should ever chance for him. He chose us himself
out of all his host for this adventure here,
expecting action; he armed me with you
because he accounted us keen under helmet,
men able with the spear – even though our lord
intended to take on this task of courage

as his own share, as shepherd of the people,
and champion of mankind in the achieving of glory
and deeds of daring.

                    That day has now come
when he stands in need of the strength of good fighters,
our lord and liege. Let us go to him,
help our leader for as long as it requires,
the fearsome fire-blast. I had far rather
that the flame should enfold my flesh-frame there
alongside my gold-giver – as God knows of me.
To bear our shields back to our homes
would seem unfitting to me, unless first we have been able
to kill the foe and defend the life
of the prince of the Weather-Geats. I well know
that former deeds deserve not that, alone
of the flower of the Geats, he should feel the pain,
sink in the struggle; sword and helmet,
corselet and mail-shirt, shall be our common gear.'

He strode through the blood-smoke, bore his war-helmet
to the aid of his lord, uttered few words:
'Beloved Beowulf, bear all things well!
You gave it out long ago in your youth
that, living, you would not allow your glory
ever to abate. Bold-tempered chieftain,
famed for your deeds, you must defend your life now
with all your strength. I shall help you.'

When these words had been spoken, the worm came on wrathful,
attacked a second time, terrible visitant,
sought out his foes in a surge of flame,
the hated men.
                    Mail-shirt did not serve
the young spear-man; and shield was withered
back to the boss by the billow of fire;
but when the blazing had burnt up his own,
the youngster stepped smartly to take
the cover of his kinsman's. Then did that kingly warrior
remember his deeds again and dealt out a sword-blow
with his full strength: it struck into the head

with annihilating weight. But Nailing snapped,
failed in the battle, Beowulf's sword
of ancient grey steel. It was not granted to him
that an iron edge could ever lend him
help in a battle; his hand was too strong.
I have heard that any sword, however hardened by wounds,
that he bore into battle, his blow would overtax
 – any weapon whatever; it was the worse for him.

A third time the terrible fire-drake
remembered the feud. The foe of the people
rushed in on the champion when a chance offered:
seething with warspite, he seized his whole neck
between bitter fangs: blood covered him,
Beowulf's life-blood, let in streams.
Then I heard how the earl alongside the king
in the hour of need made known the valour,
boldness and strength that were bred in him.
His hand burned as he helped his kinsman,
but the brave soldier in his splendid armour
ignored the head and hit the attacker
somewhat below it, so that the sword went in,
flashing-hilted; and the fire began
to slacken in consequence.
                              The king once more
took command of his wits, caught up a stabbing-knife
of the keenest battle-sharpness, that he carried in his harness:
and the Geats' Helm struck through the serpent's body.

So daring drove out life: they had downed their foe
by common action, the atheling pair,
and had made an end of him. So in the hour of need
a warrior must live. For the lord this was
the last victory in the list of his deeds
and works in the world. The wound that the earth-drake
had first succeeded in inflicting on him
began to burn and swell; he swiftly felt
the bane beginning to boil in his chest,
the poison within him. The prince walked across
to the side of the barrow, considering deeply;
he sat down on a ledge, looked at the giant-work,

saw how the age-old earth-hall contained
stone arches anchored on pillars.
Then that excellent thane with his own hands washed
his battle-bloodied prince, bathed with water
the famous leader, his friend and lord,
sated with fighting; he unfastened his helmet.

ANONYMOUS

'A Bird came down the Walk'

A Bird came down the Walk –
He did not know I saw –
He bit an Angleworm in halves
And ate the fellow, raw,

And then he drank a Dew
From a convenient Grass –
And then hopped sidewise to the Wall
To let a Beetle pass –

He glanced with rapid eyes
That hurried all around –
They looked like frightened Beads, I thought –
He stirred his Velvet Head

Like one in danger, Cautious,
I offered him a Crumb
And he unrolled his feathers
And rowed him softer home –

Than Oars divide the Ocean,
Too silver for a seam –
Or Butterflies, off Banks of Noon
Leap, plashless as they swim.

EMILY DICKINSON

Birds' Nests

The summer nests uncovered by autumn wind,
Some torn, others dislodged, all dark,
Everyone sees them: low or high in tree,
Or hedge, or single bush, they hang like a mark.

Since there's no need of eyes to see them with
I cannot help a little shame
That I missed most, even at eye's level, till
The leaves blew off and made the seeing no game.

'Tis a light pang. I like to see the nests
Still in their places, now first known,
At home and by far roads. Boys knew them not,
Whatever jays and squirrels may have done.

And most I like the winter nests deep-hid
That leaves and berries fell into:
Once a dormouse dined there on hazel-nuts,
And grass and goose-grass seeds found soil and grew.

EDWARD THOMAS

A Black November Turkey

To A. M. and A. M.

   Nine white chickens come
   With haunchy walk and heads
Jabbing among the chips, the chaff, the stones
     And the cornhusk-shreds,

   And bit by bit infringe
   A pond of dusty light,
Spectral in shadow until they bobbingly one
     By one ignite.

   Neither pale nor bright,
   The turkey-cock parades
Through radiant squalors, darkly auspicious as
     The ace of spades,

Himself his own cortège
And puffed with the pomp of death,
Rehearsing over and over with strangled râle
    His latest breath.

The vast black body floats
Above the crossing knees
As a cloud over thrashed branches, a calm ship
    Over choppy seas,

Shuddering its fan and feathers
In fine soft clashes
With the cold sound that the wind makes, fondling
    Paper-ashes.

The pale-blue bony head ,
Set on its shepherd's-crook
Like a saint's death-mask, turns a vague, superb
    And timeless look

Upon these clocking hens
And the cocks that one by one,
Dawn after mortal dawn, with vulgar joy
    Acclaim the sun.

RICHARD WILBUR

A Blessing

Just off the highway to Rochester, Minnesota,
Twilight bounds softly forth on the grass.
And the eyes of those two Indian ponies
Darken with kindness.
They have come gladly out of the willows
To welcome my friend and me.
We step over the barbed wire into the pasture
Where they have been grazing all day, alone.
They ripple tensely, they can hardly contain their happiness
That we have come.
They bow shyly as wet swans. They love each other.

There is no loneliness like theirs.
At home once more,
They begin munching the young tufts of spring in the darkness.
I would like to hold the slenderer one in my arms,
For she has walked over to me
And nuzzled my left hand.
She is black and white,
Her mane falls wild on her forehead,
And the light breeze moves me to caress her long ear
That is delicate as the skin over a girl's wrist.
Suddenly I realize
That if I stepped out of my body I would break
Into blossom.

JAMES WRIGHT

Blue Moles

I

They're out of the dark's ragbag, these two
Moles dead in the pebbled rut,
Shapeless as flung gloves, a few feet apart –
Blue suede a dog or fox has chewed.
One, by himself, seemed pitiable enough,
Little victim unearthed by some large creature
From his orbit under the elm root.
The second carcass makes a duel of the affair:
Blind twins bitten by bad nature.

The sky's far dome is sane and clear.
Leaves, undoing their yellow caves
Between the road and the lake water,
Bare no sinister spaces. Already
The moles look neutral as the stones.
Their corkscrew noses, their white hands
Uplifted, stiffen in a family pose.
Difficult to imagine how fury struck –
Dissolved now, smoke of an old war.

Nightly the battle-shouts start up
In the ear of the veteran, and again
I enter the soft pelt of the mole.
Light's death to them: they shrivel in it.
They move through their mute rooms while I sleep,
Palming the earth aside, grubbers
After the fat children of root and rock.
By day, only the topsoil heaves.
Down there one is alone.

Outsize hands prepare a path,
They go before: opening the veins,
Delving for the appendages
Of beetles, sweetbreads, shards – to be eaten
Over and over. And still the heaven
Of final surfeit is just as far
From the door as ever. What happens between us
Happens in darkness, vanishes
Easy and often as each breath.

SYLVIA PLATH

from The Book of Joel (Chapter 2)

Blow ye the trumpet in Zion, and sound an alarm in my holy mountain:
let all the inhabitants of the land tremble; for the day of the Lord
cometh, for it is nigh at hand.

A day of darkness and of gloominess, a day of clouds and of thick
darkness, as the morning spread upon the mountains: a great people
and a strong; there hath not been ever the like, neither shall be any
more after it, even to the years of many generations.

A fire devoureth before them; and behind them a flame burneth: the
land is as the garden of Eden before them, and behind them a desolate
wilderness; yea, and nothing shall escape them.

The appearance of them is as the appearance of horses; and as
horsemen so shall they run.

Like the noise of chariots on the tops of mountains they shall leap,

like the noise of a flame of fire that devoureth the stubble, as a strong
people set in battle array.

Before their face the people shall be much pained: all faces shall
gather blackness.

They shall run like mighty men; they shall climb the wall like men
of war; and they shall march every one on his ways, and they shall not
break their ranks:

Neither shall one thrust another; they shall walk every one in his
path: and when they fall upon the sword, they shall not be wounded.

They shall run to and fro in the city; they shall run upon the wall,
they shall climb up upon the houses; they shall enter in at the windows
like a thief.

The earth shall quake before them; the heavens shall tremble: the sun
and the moon shall be dark, and the stars shall withdraw their shining:

And the Lord shall utter his voice before his army: for his camp is
very great: for he is strong that executeth his word: for the day of
the Lord is great and very terrible; and who can abide it?

The Book-Worms

Through and through the inspired leaves,
   Ye maggots, make your windings;
But, oh! respect his lordship's taste,
   And spare his golden bindings.

ROBERT BURNS

The Bull Moses

A hoist up and I could lean over
The upper edge of the high half-door,
My left foot ledged on the hinge, and look in at the byre's
Blaze of darkness: a sudden shut-eyed look
Backward into the head.
                        Blackness is depth
Beyond star. But the warm weight of his breathing,

The ammoniac reek of his litter, the hotly-tongued
Mash of his cud, steamed against me.
Then, slowly, as onto the mind's eye –
The brow like masonry, the deep-keeled neck:
Something come up there onto the brink of the gulf,
Hadn't heard of the world, too deep in itself to be called to,
Stood in sleep. He would swing his muzzle at a fly
But the square of sky where I hung, shouting, waving,
Was nothing to him; nothing of our light
Found any reflection in him.

       Each dusk the farmer led him
Down to the pond to drink and smell the air,
And he took no pace but the farmer
Led him to take it, as if he knew nothing
Of the ages and continents of his fathers,
Shut, while he wombed, to a dark shed
And steps between his door and the duckpond;
The weight of the sun and the moon and the world hammered
To a ring of brass through his nostrils.

         He would raise
His streaming muzzle and look out over the meadows,
But the grasses whispered nothing awake, the fetch
Of the distance drew nothing to momentum
In the locked black of his powers. He came strolling gently back,
Paused neither toward the pig-pens on his right,
Nor toward the cow-byres on his left: something
Deliberate in his leisure, some beheld future
Founding in his quiet.

      I kept the door wide,
Closed it after him and pushed the bolt.

  TED HUGHES

Bullfrog

With their lithe long strong legs
Some frogs are able
To thump upon double-

Bass strings though pond-water deadens and clogs.

But you, bullfrog, you pump out
Whole fogs full of horn – a threat
As of a liner looming. True
That, first hearing you
Disgorging your gouts of darkness like a wounded god,
Not utterly fantastical I expected
(As in some antique tale depicted)
A broken-down bull up to its belly in mud,
Sucking black swamp up, belching out black cloud

And a squall of gudgeon and lilies.
                                        A surprise,
To see you, a boy's prize,
No bigger than a rat – all dumb silence
In your little old woman hands.

TED HUGHES

The Butterfly

I
Should I say that you're dead?
You touched so brief a fragment
of time. There's much that's sad in
        the joke God played.
        I scarcely comprehend
the words 'you've lived'; the date of
your birth and when you faded
        in my cupped hand
are one, and not two dates.
        Thus calculated,
your term is, simply stated,
        less than a day.

II
It's clear that days for us
        are nothings, zeros.

They can't be pinned down near us
to feed our eyes.
Whenever days stand stark
against white borders,
since they possess no bodies
they leave no mark.
They are like you. That is,
each butterfly's small plumage
is one day's shrunken image –
a tenth its size.

III

Should I say that, somehow,
you lack all being?
What, then, are my hands feeling
that's so like you?
Such colors can't be drawn
from nonexistence.
Tell me, at whose insistence
were yours laid on?
Since I'm a mumbling heap
of words, not pigments,
how could your hues be figments
of my conceit?

IV

There are, on your small wings,
black spots and splashes –
like eyes, birds, girls, eyelashes.
But of what things
are you the airy norm?
What bits of faces,
what broken times and places
shine through your form?
As for your *nature mortes*:
do they show dishes
of fruits and flowers, or fishes
displayed on boards?

V

Perhaps a landscape smokes
among your ashes,
and with thick reading glasses
I'll scan its slopes –
its beaches, dancers, nymphs.
Is it as bright as
the day, or dark as night is?
and could one glimpse –
ascending that sky's screen –
some blazing lantern?
And tell me, please, what pattern
inspired this scene?

VI

It seems to me you are
a protean creature,
whose markings mask a feature
of face, or stone, or star.
Who was the jeweler,
brow uncontracted,
who from our world extracted
your miniature –
a world where madness brings
us low, and lower,
where we are things, while you are
the thought of things?

VII

Why were these lovely shapes
and colors given
for your one day of life in
this land of lakes?
– a land whose dappled mirrors have one merit:
reflecting space, they store it.
Such brief existence tore
away your chance
to be captured, delivered,

within cupped hands to quiver –
the hunter's eye entrance.

VIII

You shun every response –
but not from shyness
or wickedness or slyness,
and not because
you're dead. Dead or alive,
to God's least creature
is given voice for speech, or
for song – a sign
that it has found a way
to bind together,
and stretch life's limits, whether
an hour or day.

IX

But you lack even this:
the means to utter
a word. Yet, probe the matter;
it's better thus.
You're not in heaven's debt,
on heaven's ledger.
It's not a curse, I pledge you,
that your small weight
and span rob you of tongue.
Sound's burden, too, is grievous.
And you're more speechless,
less fleshed, than time.

X

Living too brief an hour
for fear or trembling,
you spin, motelike, ascending
above this bed of flowers,
beyond the prison space
where past and future
combine to break, or batter,
our lives, and thus

when your path leads you far
to open meadows,
your pulsing wings bring shadows
and shapes to air.

XI
So, too, the sliding pen
which inks a surface
has no sense of the purpose
of any line
or that the whole will end
as an amalgam
of heresy and wisdom;
it therefore trusts the hand
whose silent speech incites
fingers to throbbing –
whose spasm reaps no pollen,
but eases hearts.

XII
Such beauty, set beside
so brief a season,
suggests to our stunned reason
this bleak surmise:
the world was made to hold
no end or *telos*,
and if – as some would tell us –
there is a goal,
it's not ourselves.
No butterfly collector
can trap light or detect where
the darkness dwells.

XIII
Should I bid you farewell
as to a day that's over?
Men's memories may wither,
grow thin, and fall
like hair. The trouble is,
behind their backs are:
not double beds for lovers,

            hard sleep, the past,
        or days in shrinking files
    backstretched – but, rather,
huge clouds, circling together,
            of butterflies.

                    XIV
You're better than No-thing.
        That is, you're nearer,
more reachable, and clearer.
            Yet you're akin
            to nothingness –
like it, you're wholly empty.
And if, in your life's venture,
        No-thing takes flesh,
            that flesh will die.
Yet while you live you offer
    a frail and shifting buffer,
        dividing it from me.

    JOSEPH BRODSKY
    Translated from the Russian by George L. Kline

Cape Ann

O quick quick quick, quick hear the song-sparrow,
Swamp-sparrow, fox-sparrow, vesper-sparrow
At dawn and dusk. Follow the dance
Of the goldfinch at noon. Leave to chance
The Blackburnian warbler, the shy one. Hail
With shrill whistle the note of the quail, the bob-white
Dodging by bay-bush. Follow the feet
Of the walker, the water-thrush. Follow the flight
Of the dancing arrow, the purple martin. Greet
In silence the bullbat. All are delectable. Sweet sweet sweet
But resign this land at the end, resign it
To its true owner, the tough one, the sea-gull.
The palaver is finished.

    T. S. ELIOT

The Captiv'd Bee: or, The Little Filcher

As Julia once a-slumb'ring lay,
It chanc't a Bee did flie that way,
(After a dew, or dew-like shower)
To tipple freely in a flower.
For some rich flower, he took the lip
Of Julia, and began to sip;
But when he felt he suckt from thence
Hony, and in the quintessence;
He drank so much he scarce co'd stir;
So Julia took the pilferer.
And thus surpriz'd (as Filchers use)
He thus began himselfe t' excuse:
Sweet Lady-Flower, I never brought
Hither the least one theeving thought:
But taking those rare lips of yours
For some fresh, fragrant, luscious flowers:
I thought I might there take a taste,
Where so much sirrop ran at waste.
Besides, know this, I never sting
The flower that gives me nourishing:
But with a kisse, or thanks, doe pay
For Honie, that I beare away.
This said, he laid his little scrip
Of hony, 'fore her Ladiship:
And told her, (as some tears did fall)
That that, he took, and that was all.
At which she smil'd; and bade him goe
And take his bag; but thus much know,
When next he came a-pilfring so,
He sho'd from her full lips derive,
Hony enough to fill his hive.

ROBERT HERRICK

The Cat and the Fiddle

   Hey diddle, diddle,
    The cat and the fiddle,
The cow jumped over the moon;
    The little dog laughed
    To see such sport,
And the dish ran away with the spoon.

ANONYMOUS

The Cat and the Moon

The cat went here and there
And the moon spun round like a top,
And the nearest kin of the moon,
The creeping cat, looked up.
Black Minnaloushe stared at the moon,
For, wander and wail as he would,
The pure cold light in the sky
Troubled his animal blood.
Minnaloushe runs in the grass
Lifting his delicate feet.
Do you dance, Minnaloushe, do you dance?
When two close kindred meet,
What better than call a dance?
Maybe the moon may learn,
Tired of that courtly fashion,
A new dance turn.
Minnaloushe creeps through the grass
From moonlit place to place,
The sacred moon overhead
Has taken a new phase.
Does Minnaloushe know that his pupils
Will pass from change to change,
And that from round to crescent,
From crescent to round they range?
Minnaloushe creeps through the grass

Alone, important and wise,
And lifts to the changing moon
His changing eyes.

W. B. YEATS

Celia Upon Her Sparrow

Tell me not of joy: there's none
Now my little Sparrow's gone;
 He, just as you
 Would toy and woo,
He would chirp and flatter me,
He would hang the wing awhile,
Till at length he saw me smile,
Lord, how sullen he would be!

He would catch a crumb, and then
Sporting let it go again,
 He from my lip
 Would moisture sip.
He would from my trencher feed,
Then would hop, and then would run
And cry *Philip* when h' had done,
O whose heart can choose but bleed?

O how eager would he fight
And ne'er hurt though he bite;
 No morn did pass
 But on my glass
He would sit and mark and do
What I did, now ruffle all
His feathers o'er, now let 'em fall
And then straightway sleek them too.

Whence will Cupid get his darts
Feathered now to pierce our hearts?
 A wound he may
 Not Love convey.

Now this faithful bird is gone,
O let mournful turtles join
With loving red-breasts, and combine,
    To sing dirges o'er his stone.

    WILLIAM CARTWRIGHT

Champagne

The soulless matchmaking of lunar moths,
Uncanny, delicate or helpful, dove-coloured
Bosoms in the night: their fictions hurt us
Gently, like the nudity of rose-beige tea-gowns . . .

The mayflies' opera is their only moon, only
Those that fall on water reproduce, content
With scattering in fog or storm, such ivory
As elephants hold lofty, like champagne.

    MEDBH MCGUCKIAN

from Childe Harold's Pilgrimage (Canto 1)

All have their fooleries – not alike are thine,
Fair Cadiz, rising o'er the dark blue sea!
Soon as the matin bell proclaimeth nine,
Thy saint adorers count the rosary:
Much is the VIRGIN teaz'd to shrive them free
(Well do I ween the only virgin there)
From crimes as numerous as her beadsmen be;
Then to the crowded circus forth they fare,
Young, old, high, low, at once the same diversion share.

The lists are op'd, the spacious area clear'd,
Thousands on thousands pil'd are seated round;
Long ere the first loud trumpet's note is heard,
Ne vacant space for lated wight is found:

Here dons, grandees, but chiefly dames abound,
Skill'd in the ogle of a roguish eye,
Yet ever well inclin'd to heal the wound;
None through their cold disdain are doom'd to die,
As moon-struck bards complain, by Love's sad archery.

Hush'd is the din of tongues – on gallant steeds,
With milk-white crest, gold spur, and light-pois'd lance,
Four cavaliers prepare for venturous deeds,
And lowly bending to the lists advance;
Rich are their scarfs, their chargers featly prance:
If in the dangerous game they shine to-day,
The crowds loud shout and ladies lovely glance,
Best prize of better acts, they bear away,
And all that kings or chiefs e'er gain their toils repay.

In costly sheen and gaudy cloak array'd,
But all afoot, the light-limb'd Matadore
Stands in the centre, eager to invade
The lord of lowing herds; but not before
The ground, with cautious tread, is travers'd o'er,
Lest aught unseen should lurk to thwart his speed:
His arms a dart, he fights aloof, nor more
Can man achieve without the friendly steed,
Alas! too oft condemn'd for him to bear and bleed.

Thrice sounds the clarion; lo! the signal falls,
The den expands, and Expectation mute
Gapes round the silent Circle's peopled walls.
Bounds with one lashing spring the mighty brute,
And, wildly staring, spurns, with sounding foot,
The sand, nor blindly rushes on his foe:
Here, there, he points his threatening front to suit
His first attack, wide waving to and fro
His angry tail; red rolls his eye's dilated glow.

Sudden he stops; his eye is fix'd: away,
Away, thou heedless boy! prepare the spear:
Now is thy time, to perish, or display
The skill that yet may check his mad career.
With well-tim'd croupe the nimble coursers veer;
On foams the bull, but not unscath'd he goes;

53 /

Streams from his flank the crimson torrent clear:
He flies, he wheels, distracted with his throes;
Dart follows dart; lance, lance; loud bellowings speak his woes.

Again he comes; nor dart nor lance avail,
Nor the wild plunging of the tortur'd horse;
Though man and man's avenging arms assail,
Vain are his weapons, vainer is his force.
One gallant steed is stretch'd a mangled corse;
Another, hideous sight! unseam'd appears,
His gory chest unveils life's panting source,
Tho' death-struck still his feeble frame he rears,
Staggering, but stemming all, his lord unharm'd he bears.

Foil'd, bleeding, breathless, furious to the last,
Full in the centre stands the bull at bay,
Mid wounds, and clinging darts, and lances brast,
And foes disabled in the brutal fray:
And now the Matadores around him play,
Shake the red cloak, and poise the ready brand:
Once more through all he bursts his thundering way –
Vain rage! the mantle quits the conynge hand,
Wraps his fierce eye – 'tis past – he sinks upon the sand!

Where his vast neck just mingles with the spine,
Sheath'd in his form the deadly weapon lies.
He stops – he starts – disdaining to decline:
Slowly he falls, amidst triumphant cries,
Without a groan, without a struggle dies.
The decorated car appears – on high
The corse is pil'd – sweet sight for vulgar eyes –
Four steeds that spurn the rein, as swift as shy,
Hurl the dark bulk along, scarce seen in dashing by.

LORD BYRON

/ 54

Clock a Clay

In the cowslips peeps I lye
Hidden from the buzzing fly
While green grass beneath me lies
Pearled wi' dew like fishes eyes
Here I lye a Clock a clay
Waiting for the time o' day

While grassy forests quake surprise
And the wild wind sobs and sighs
My gold home rocks as like to fall
On its pillars green and tall
When the pattering rain drives bye
Clock a Clay keeps warm and dry

Day by day and night by night
All the week I hide from sight
In the cowslips peeps I lye
In rain and dew still warm and dry
Day and night and night and day
Red black spotted clock a clay

My home it shakes in wind and showers
Pale green pillar top't wi' flowers
Bending at the wild winds breath
Till I touch the grass beneath
Here still I live lone clock a clay
Watching for the time of day

JOHN CLARE

Cock-Crow

Out of the wood of thoughts that grows by night
To be cut down by the sharp axe of light, –
Out of the night, two cocks together crow,
Cleaving the darkness with a silver blow:
And bright before my eyes twin trumpeters stand,

Heralds of splendour, one at either hand,
Each facing each as in a coat of arms:
The milkers lace their boots up at the farms.

EDWARD THOMAS

Cock-Crowing

Father of lights! What sunny seed,
What glance of day hast thou confined
Into this bird? To all the breed
This busy ray thou hast assigned;
   Their magnetism works all night,
   And dreams of Paradise and light.

Their eyes watch for the morning-hue,
Their little grain, expelling night,
So shines and sings, as if it knew
The path unto the house of light.
   It seems their candle, howe'er done,
   Was tined and lighted at the sun.

If such a tincture, such a touch,
So firm a longing can impower,
Shall thy own image think it much
To watch for thy appearing hour?
   If a mere blast so fill the sail,
   Shall not the breath of God prevail?

O thou immortal light and heat,
Whose hand so shines through all this frame,
That by the beauty of the seat
We plainly see who made the same;
   Seeing thy seed abides in me,
   Dwell thou in it, and I in thee!

To sleep without thee is to die;
Yea, 'tis a death partakes of hell:
For where thou dost not close the eye,

It never opens, I can tell.
    In such a dark, Egyptian border
    The shades of death dwell, and disorder.

If joys, and hopes, and earnest throes,
And hearts, whose pulse beats still for light
Are given to birds: who, but thee, knows
A love-sick soul's exalted flight?
    Can souls be tracked by any eye
    But his, who gave them wings to fly?

Only this veil which thou hast broke,
And must be broken yet in me,
This veil, I say, is all the cloak,
And cloud which shadows thee from me.
    This veil thy full-eyed love denies,
    And only gleams and fractions spies.

O take it off! Make no delay,
But brush me with thy light, that I
May shine unto a perfect day,
And warm me at thy glorious eye!
    O take it off! or till it flee,
    Though with no lily, stay with me!

HENRY VAUGHAN

Cock Robin

Who killed Cock Robin?
I, said the Sparrow,
With my bow and arrow,
I killed Cock Robin.

Who saw him die?
I, said the Fly,
With my little eye,
I saw him die.

Who caught his blood?

I, said the Fish,
With my little dish,
I caught his blood.

Who'll make his shroud?
I, said the Beetle,
With my thread and needle,
I'll make the shroud.

Who'll dig his grave?
I, said the Owl,
With my pick and shovel,
I'll dig his grave.

Who'll be the parson?
I, said the Rook,
With my little book,
I'll be the parson.

Who'll be the clerk?
I, said the Lark,
If it's not in the dark,
I'll be the clerk.

Who'll carry the link?
I, said the Linnet,
I'll fetch it in a minute,
I'll carry the link.

Who'll be chief mourner?
I, said the Dove,
I mourn for my love,
I'll be chief mourner.

Who'll carry the coffin?
I, said the Kite,
If it's not through the night
I'll carry the coffin.

Who'll bear the pall?
We, said the Wren,
Both the cock and the hen,
We'll bear the pall.

Who'll sing a psalm?
I, said the Thrush,
As she sat on a bush,
I'll sing a psalm.

Who'll toll the bell?
I, said the Bull,
Because I can pull,
I'll toll the bell.

All the birds of the air
Fell a-sighing and a-sobbing,
When they heard the bell toll
For poor Cock Robin.

ANONYMOUS

The Collar-Bone of a Hare

Would I could cast a sail on the water
Where many a king has gone
And many a king's daughter,
And alight at the comely trees and the lawn,
The playing upon pipes and the dancing,
And learn that the best thing is
To change my loves while dancing
And pay but a kiss for a kiss.

I would find by the edge of that water
The collar-bone of a hare
Worn thin by the lapping of water,
And pierce it through with a gimlet, and stare
At the old bitter world where they marry in churches,
And laugh over the untroubled water
At all who marry in churches,
Through the white thin bone of a hare.

W. B. YEATS

The Combe

The Combe was ever dark, ancient and dark.
Its mouth is stopped with bramble, thorn, and briar;
And no one scrambles over the sliding chalk
By beech and yew and perishing juniper
Down the half precipices of its sides, with roots
And rabbit holes for steps. The sun of Winter,
The moon of Summer, and all the singing birds
Except the missel-thrush that loves juniper,
Are quite shut out. But far more ancient and dark
The Combe looks since they killed the badger there,
Dug him out and gave him to the hounds,
That most ancient Briton of English beasts.

EDWARD THOMAS

Come In

As I came to the edge of the woods,
Thrush music – hark!
Now if it was dusk outside,
Inside it was dark.

Too dark in the woods for a bird
By sleight of wing
To better its perch for the night,
Though it still could sing.

The last of the light of the sun
That had died in the west
Still lived for one song more
In a thrush's breast.

Far in the pillared dark
Thrush music went –
Almost like a call to come in
To the dark and lament.

But no, I was out for stars:

I would not come in.
I meant not even if asked,
And I hadn't been.

ROBERT FROST

Considering the Snail

The snail pushes through a green
night, for the grass is heavy
with water and meets over
the bright path he makes, where rain
has darkened the earth's dark. He
moves in a wood of desire,

pale antlers barely stirring
as he hunts. I cannot tell
what power is at work, drenched there
with purpose, knowing nothing.
What is a snail's fury? All
I think is that if later

I parted the blades above
the tunnel and saw the thin
trail of broken white across
litter, I would never have
imagined the slow passion
to that deliberate progress.

THOM GUNN

The Cow in Apple Time

Something inspires the only cow of late
To make no more of a wall than an open gate,
And think no more of wall-builders than fools.
Her face is flecked with pomace and she drools

A cider syrup. Having tasted fruit,
She scorns a pasture withering to the root.
She runs from tree to tree where lie and sweeten
The windfalls spiked with stubble and worm-eaten.
She leaves them bitten when she has to fly.
She bellows on a knoll against the sky.
Her udder shrivels and the milk goes dry.

ROBERT FROST

Cow in Calf

It seems she has swallowed a barrel.
From forelegs to haunches
her belly is slung like a hammock.

Slapping her out of the byre is like slapping
a great bag of seed. My hand
tingled as if strapped, but I had to
hit her again and again and
heard the blows plump like a depth-charge
far in her gut.

The udder grows. Windbags
of bagpipes are crammed there
to drone in her lowing.
Her cud and her milk, her heats and her calves
keep coming and going.

SEAMUS HEANEY

The Crocodile

Now listen you landsmen unto me, to tell you the truth I'm bound,
What happened to me by going to sea, and the wonders that I found;
Shipwrecked I was once off Perouse and cast upon the shore,

So then I did resolve to roam, the country to explore.
  Tomy rit fal lal li bollem tit, tomy rit fal lal li dee!
  Tomy rit fal lal li bollem tit, tomy rit fal lal li dee!

'Twas far I had not scouted out, when close along-side the ocean,
I saw something move which at first I thought was all the world in
    motion;
But steering up close alongside, I found 'twas a crocodile,
And from his nose to the tip of his tail he measured five hundred mile.
  Tomy rit, etc.

While up aloft the wind was high, it blew a gale from the south,
I lost my hold and away did fly right into the crocodile's mouth,
He quickly closed his jaws on me and thought he'd got a victim,
But I ran down his throat, d'ye see, and that's the way I tricked him.
  Tomy rit, etc.

I travelled on for a month or two, till I got into his maw,
Where I found of rum-kegs not a few, and a thousand fat bullocks in
    store,
Of life I banished all my care, for of grub I was not stinted,
And in this crocodile I lived ten years, and very well contented.
  Tomy rit, etc.

This crocodile being very old, one day, alas, he died;
He was ten long years a-getting cold, he was so long and wide.
His skin was eight miles thick, I'm sure, or very near about,
For I was full ten years or more a-cutting my way out.
  Tomy rit, etc.

And now I've once more got on earth, I've vow'd no more to roam,
In a ship that passed I got a berth, and now I'm safe at home.
And if my story you should doubt, should you ever travel the Nile,
It's ten to one you'll find the shell of the wonderful crocodile.
  Tomy rit, etc.

ANONYMOUS

The Cuckoo

In the month of Averil
the gowk comes over the hill
in a shower of rain

ANONYMOUS

The Cuckoo

O the cuckoo she's a pretty bird,
  She singeth as she flies,
She bringeth good tidings,
  She telleth no lies.

She sucketh white flowers
  For to keep her voice clear,
And the more she singeth cuckoo
  The summer draweth near.

ANONYMOUS

The Cuckoo Song

  Sing, cuccu, nu. Sing, cuccu.
  Sing, cuccu. Sing, cuccu, nu.

Sumer is i-cumen in –
  Lhude sing, cuccu!
Groweth sed and bloweth med
  And springth the wude nu.
    Sing, cuccu!

Awe bleteth after lomb,
  Lhouth after calve cu,
Bulluc sterteth, bucke verteth –
  Murie sing, cuccu!

Cuccu, cuccu.
Wel singes thu, cuccu.
Ne swik thu naver nu!

ANONYMOUS

Cynthia on Horseback

Fair Cynthia mounted on her sprightly pad,
Which in white robe with silver fringe was clad,
   And swift as wind his graceful steps did move,
   As with his beauteous guide he'd been in love.
Though fierce, yet humble still to her command,
Obeying ev'ry touch of her fair hand;
   Her golden bit his foaming mouth did check,
   It spread his crest, and rais'd his bending neck.

She was the rose upon this hill of snow,
Her sparkling beauty made this glorious show;
   Whence secret flames men in their bosoms took:
The Graces and the Cupids her surround,
Attending her, while cruel she does wound,
   With switch her horse, and hearts with ev'ry look.

PHILIP AYRES

The Dalliance of the Eagles

Skirting the river road, (my forenoon walk, my rest,)
Skyward in air a sudden muffled sound, the dalliance of the eagles,
The rushing amorous contact high in space together,
The clinching interlocking claws, a living, fierce, gyrating wheel,
Four beating wings, two beaks, a swirling mass tight grappling,
In tumbling turning clustering loops, straight downward falling,
Till o'er the river pois'd, the twain yet one, a moment's lull,
A motionless still balance in the air, then parting, talons loosing,

Upward again on slow-firm pinions slanting, their separate diverse
    flight,
She hers, he his, pursuing.

    WALT WHITMAN

The Darkling Thrush

I leant upon a coppice gate
    When Frost was spectre-gray,
And Winter's dregs made desolate
    The weakening eye of day.
The tangled bine-stems scored the sky
    Like strings of broken lyres,
And all mankind that haunted nigh
    Had sought their household fires.

The land's sharp features seemed to be
    The Century's corpse outleant,
His crypt the cloudy canopy,
    The wind his death-lament.
The ancient pulse of germ and birth
    Was shrunken hard and dry,
And every spirit upon earth
    Seemed fervourless as I.

At once a voice arose among
    The bleak twigs overhead
In a full-hearted evensong
    Of joy illimited;
An aged thrush, frail, gaunt, and small,
    In blast-beruffled plume,
Had chosen thus to fling his soul
    Upon the growing gloom.

So little cause for carolings
    Of such ecstatic sound
Was written on terrestrial things
    Afar or nigh around,

That I could think there trembled through
   His happy good-night air
Some blessed Hope, whereof he knew
   And I was unaware.

   THOMAS HARDY

Death of a Naturalist

All year the flax-dam festered in the heart
Of the townland; green and heavy headed
Flax had rotted there, weighted down by huge sods.
Daily it sweltered in the punishing sun.
Bubbles gargled delicately, bluebottles
Wove a strong gauze of sound around the smell.
There were dragon-flies, spotted butterflies,
But best of all was the warm thick slobber
Of frogspawn that grew like clotted water
In the shade of the banks. Here, every spring
I would fill jampotfuls of the jellied
Specks to range on window-sills at home,
On shelves at school, and wait and watch until
The fattening dots burst into nimble-
Swimming tadpoles. Miss Walls would tell us how
The daddy frog was called a bullfrog
And how he croaked and how the mammy frog
Laid hundreds of little eggs and this was
Frogspawn. You could tell the weather by frogs too
For they were yellow in the sun and brown
In rain.

   Then one hot day when fields were rank
With cowdung in the grass the angry frogs
Invaded the flax-dam; I ducked through hedges
To a coarse croaking that I had not heard
Before. The air was thick with a bass chorus.
Right down the dam gross-bellied frogs were cocked
On sods; their loose necks pulsed like sails. Some hopped:

The slap and plop were obscene threats. Some sat
Poised like mud grenades, their blunt heads farting.
I sickened, turned, and ran. The great slime kings
Were gathered there for vengeance and I knew
That if I dipped my hand the spawn would clutch it.

SEAMUS HEANEY

The Death of a Toad

A toad the power mower caught,
Chewed and clipped of a leg, with a hobbling hop has got
   To the garden verge, and sanctuaried him
   Under the cineraria leaves, in the shade
     Of the ashen heartshaped leaves, in a dim,
       Low, and a final glade.

The rare original heartsblood goes,
Spends on the earthen hide, in the folds and wizenings, flows
   In the gutters of the banked and staring eyes. He lies
   As still as if he would return to stone,
     And soundlessly attending, dies
       Toward some deep monotone,

Toward misted and ebullient seas
And cooling shores, toward lost Amphibia's emperies.
   Day dwindles, drowning, and at length is gone
   In the wide and antique eyes, which still appear
     To watch, across the castrate lawn,
       The haggard daylight steer.

RICHARD WILBUR

Dehorning

Bad-tempered bullying bunch, the horned cows
Among the unhorned. Feared, spoilt.

Cantankerous at the hay, at assemblies, at crowded
Yard operations. Knowing their horn-tips' position
To a fraction, every other cow knowing it too,
Like their own tenderness. Horning of bellies, hair-tufting
Of horn-tips. Handy levers. But
Off with the horns.
So there they all are in the yard –
The pick of the bullies, churning each other
Like thick fish in a bucket, churning their mud.
One by one, into the cage of the crush: the needle,
A roar not like a cow – more like a tiger,
Blast of air down a cavern, and long, long
Beginning in pain and ending in terror – then the next.
The needle between the horn and the eye, so deep
Your gut squirms for the eyeball twisting
In its pink-white fastenings of tissue. This side and that.
Then the first one anaesthetised, back in the crush.
The bulldog pincers in the septum, stretched full strength,
The horn levered right over, the chin pulled round
With the pincers, the mouth drooling, the eye
Like a live eye caught in a pan, like the eye of a fish
Imprisoned in air. Then the cheese cutter
Of braided wire, and stainless steel peg handles,
Aligned on the hair-bedded root of the horn, then leaning
Backward full weight, pull-punching backwards,
Left right left right and the blood leaks
Down over the cheekbone, the wire bites
And buzzes, the ammonia horn-burn smokes
And the cow groans, roars shapelessly, hurls
Its half-ton commotion in the tight cage. Our faces
Grimace like faces in the dentist's chair. The horn
Rocks from its roots, the wire pulls through
The last hinge of hair, the horn is heavy and free,
And a water-pistol jet of blood
Rains over the one who holds it – a needle jet
From the white-rasped and bloody skull-crater. Then tweezers
Twiddle the artery nozzle, knotting it enough,
And purple antiseptic squirts a cuttlefish cloud over it.
Then the other side the same. We collect
A heap of horns. The floor of the crush

Is a trampled puddle of scarlet. The purple-crowned cattle,
The bullies, with suddenly no horns to fear,
Start ramming and wrestling. Maybe their heads
Are still anaesthetised. A new order
Among the hornless. The bitchy high-headed
Straight-back brindle, with her Spanish bull trot,
And her head-shaking snorting advance and her crazy spirit,
Will have to get maternal. What she's lost
In weapons, she'll have to make up for in tits.
But they've all lost one third of their beauty.

TED HUGHES

Ding, Dong, Bell

Ding, dong, bell,
Pussy's in the well.
Who put her in?
Little Johnny Green.
Who pulled her out?
Little Tommy Stout.
What a naughty boy was that
To try to drown poor pussycat,
Who never did him any harm,
But killed the mice in his father's barn.

ANONYMOUS

The Dog

Except for the dog, that she wouldn't have him put away, wouldn't let
    him die, I'd have liked her.
She was handsome, busty, chunky, early middle-aged, very black, with
    a stiff, exotic dignity
that flurried up in me a mix of warmth and sexual apprehension neither
    of which, to tell the truth,

I tried very hard to nail down: she was that much older and in those
    days there was still the race thing.
This was just at the time of civil rights: the neighborhood I was living
    in was mixed.
In the narrow streets, the tiny three-floored houses they called father-
    son-holy-ghosts
which had been servants' quarters first, workers' tenements, then slums,
    still were, but enclaves of us,
beatniks and young artists, squatted there and commerce between
    everyone was fairly easy.
Her dog, a grinning mongrel, rib and knob, gristle and grizzle, wasn't
    terribly offensive.
The trouble was that he was ill, or the trouble more exactly was that
    I had to know about it.
She used to walk him on a lot I overlooked, he must have had a tumor
    or a blockage of some sort
because every time he moved his bowels, he shrieked, a chilling, almost
    human scream of anguish.
It nearly always caught me unawares, but even when I'd see them first,
    it wasn't better.
The limp leash coiled in her hand, the woman would be profiled to
    the dog, staring into the distance,
apparently oblivious, those breasts of hers like stone, while he, not a
    step away, laboring,
trying to eject the feeble, mucus-coated, blood-flecked chains that
    finally spurted from him,
would set himself on tiptoe and hump into a question mark, one
    quivering back leg grotesquely lifted.
Every other moment he'd turn his head, as thought he wanted her, to
    no avail, to look at him,
then his eyes would dim and he'd drive his wounded anus in the dirt,
    keening uncontrollably,
lurching forward in a hideous, electric dance as though someone were
    at him with a club.
When at last he'd finish, she'd wipe him with a tissue like a child; he'd
    lick her hand.
It was horrifying; I was always going to call the police; once I actually
    went out to chastise her –
didn't she know how selfish she was, how the animal was suffering? –
    she scared me off, though.

She was older than I'd thought, for one thing, her flesh was loosening,
   pouches of fat beneath the eyes,
and poorer, too, shabby, tarnished: I imagined smelling something
   faintly acrid as I passed.
Had I ever really mooned for such a creature? I slunk around the
   block, chagrined, abashed.
I don't recall them too long after that. Maybe the dog died, maybe I
   was just less sensitive.
Maybe one year when the cold came and I closed my windows, I forgot
   them . . . then I moved.
Everything was complicated now, so many tensions, so much
   bothersome self-consciousness.
Anyway, those back streets, especially in bad weather when the ginkgos
   lost their leaves, were bleak.
It's restored there now, ivy, pointed brick, garden walls with broken
   bottles mortared on them,
but you'd get sick and tired then: the rubbish in the gutter, the general
   sense of dereliction.
Also, I'd found a girl to be in love with: all we wanted was to live
   together, so we did.

   C. K. WILLIAMS

A Dog After Love

After you left me
I let a dog smell at
My chest and my belly. It will fill its nose
And set out to find you.

I hope it will tear the
Testicles of your lover and bite off his penis
Or at least
Will bring me your stockings between his teeth.

   YEHUDA AMICHAI
   Translated from the Hebrew by the author and Ted Hughes

Dogs in the Park

The precise yet furtive etiquette of dogs
Makes them ignore the whistle while they talk
In circles round each other, one-man bonds
Deferred in pauses of this man-made walk
To open vistas to a past of packs

That raven round the stuccoed terraces
And scavenge at the mouth of Stone Age caves;
What man proposes dog on his day disposes
In litter round both human and canine graves,
Then lifts his leg to wash the gravestones clean,

While simultaneously his eyes express
Apology and contempt; his master calls
And at the last and sidelong he returns,
Part heretic, part hack, and jumps and crawls
And fumbles to communicate and fails.

And then they leave the park, the leads are snapped
On to the spiky collars, the tails wag
For no known reason and the ears are pricked
To search through legendary copse and crag
For legendary creatures doomed to die
Even as they, the dogs, were doomed to live.

LOUIS MACNEICE

The Donkey

When fishes flew and forests walked
    And figs grew upon thorn,
Some moment when the moon was blood,
    Then surely I was born;

With monstrous head and sickening cry
    And ears like errant wings,
The devil's walking parody
    On all four-footed things.

The tattered outlaw of the earth,
   Of ancient crooked will;
Starve, scourge, deride me: I am dumb,
   I keep my secret still.

Fools! For I also had my hour,
   One far fierce hour and sweet:
There was a shout about my ears,
   And palms before my feet!

   G. K. CHESTERTON

The Draft Horse

With a lantern that wouldn't burn
In too frail a buggy we drove
Behind too heavy a horse
Through a pitch-dark limitless grove.

And a man came out of the trees
And took our horse by the head
And reaching back to his ribs
Deliberately stabbed him dead.

The ponderous beast went down
With a crack of a broken shaft.
And the night drew through the trees
In one long invidious draft.

The most unquestioning pair
That ever accepted fate
And the least disposed to ascribe
Any more than we had to to hate,

We assumed that the man himself
Or someone he had to obey
Wanted us to get down
And walk the rest of the way.

   ROBERT FROST

from The Duchess of Malfi

Sad tales befit my woe: I'll tell you one.
A Salmon, as she swam unto the sea,
Met with a Dog-fish; who encounters her
With this rough language: 'Why art thou so bold
To mix thyself with our high state of floods
Being no eminent courtier, but one
That for the calmest and fresh time o'th' year
Dost live in shallow rivers, rank'st thyself
With silly Smelts and Shrimps? And darest thou
Pass by our Dog-ship without reverence?'
'O', quoth the Salmon, 'sister, be at peace:
Thank Jupiter, we both have pass'd the Net,
Our value never can be truly known,
Till in the Fisher's basket we be shown;
I'th' Market then my price may be the higher,
Even when I am nearest to the Cook, and fire.
So, to great men, the moral may be stretched.
Men oft are valued high, when th'are most wretch'd.
But come: whither you please. I am arm'd 'gainst misery:
Bent to all sways of the oppressor's will.
There's no deep valley, but near some great hill.

JOHN WEBSTER

The Eagle

Fragment

He clasps the crag with crooked hands;
Close to the sun in lonely lands,
Ring'd with the azure world, he stands.

The wrinkled sea beneath him crawls;
He watches from his mountain walls,
And like a thunderbolt he falls.

ALFRED LORD TENNYSON

An Eel

The strange part is his head. Her head. The strangely ripened
Domes over the brain, swollen nacelles
For some large containment. Lobed glands
Of some large awareness. Eerie the eel's head.
This full, plum-sleeked fruit of evolution.
Beneath it, her snout's a squashed slipper-face,
The mouth grin-long and perfunctory,
Undershot predatory. And the iris, dirty gold
Distilled only enough to be different
From the olive lode of her body,
The grained and woven blacks. And ringed larger
With a vaguer vision, an earlier eye
Behind her eye, paler, blinder,
Inward. Her buffalo hump
Begins the amazement of her progress.
Her mid-shoulder pectoral fin – concession
To fish-life – secretes itself
Flush with her concealing suit: under it
The skin's a pale exposure of deepest eel
As her belly is, a dulled pearl.
Strangest, the thumb-print skin, the rubberized weave
Of her insulation. Her whole body
Damascened with identity. This is she
Suspends the Sargasso
In her inmost hope. Her life is a cell
Sealed from event, her patience
Global and furthered with love
By the bending stars as if she
Were earth's sole initiate. Alone
In her millions, the moon's pilgrim,
The nun of water.

TED HUGHES

The Elephant *or*, The Parliament Man

Written many years since, and taken out of Coke's Institutes

E'er bribes convince you whom to choose,
The precepts of Lord Coke peruse.
Observe an elephant, says he,
And let like him your member be:
First take a man that's free from gall:
For elephants have none at all.
In flocks, or parties, must he keep:
For elephants live just like sheep.
Stubborn in honour must he be:
For elephants ne'er bend the knee.
Last, let his memory be sound,
In which your elephant's profound;
That old examples from the wise
May prompt him in his noes and ayes.

    Thus, the Lord Coke hath gravely writ,
In all the form of lawyer's wit:
And then with Latin, and all that,
Shows the comparison is pat.
Yet in some points my Lord is wrong,
One's teeth are sold, and t'other's tongue:
Now, men of parliament, God knows,
Are more like elephants of shows;
Whose docile memory and sense
Are turned to trick, to gather pence;
To get their master half a crown,
They spread the flag, or lay it down:
Those who bore bulwarks on their backs,
And guarded nations from attacks,
Now practise every pliant gesture,
Opening their trunk for every tester.
Siam, for elephants so famed,

Is not with England to be named:
Their elephants by men are sold;
Ours sell themselves, and take the gold.

JONATHAN SWIFT

Elephants

Tonnage of instinctive
Wisdom in tinsel,
Trunks like questions
And legs like tree trunks

On each forehead
A buxom blonde
And round each leg
A jangle of bells,

Deep in each brain
A chart of tropic
Swamp and twilight
Of creepered curtains,

Shamble in shoddy
Finery forward
And make their salaams
To the tiers of people –

Dummies with a reflex
Muscle of laughter
When they see the mountains
Come to Mahomet ...

Efficacy of engines,
Obstinacy of darkness.

LOUIS MACNEICE

Elephants

Uplifted and waved till immobilized
wistaria-like, the opposing opposed
mouse-gray twined proboscises' trunk formed by two
trunks, fights itself to a spiraled inter-nosed

deadlock of dyke-enforced massiveness. It's a
knock-down drag-out fight that asks no quarter? Just
a pastime, as when the trunk rains on itself
the pool it siphoned up; or when – since each must

provide his forty-pound bough dinner – he broke
the leafy branches. These templars of the Tooth,
these matched intensities, take master care of
master tools. One, sleeping with the calm of youth,

at full length in the half-dry sun-flecked stream-bed,
rests his hunting-horn-curled trunk on shallowed stone.
The sloping hollow of the sleeper's body
cradles the gently breathing eminence's prone

mahout, asleep like a lifeless six-foot
frog, so feather light the elephant's stiff
ear's unconscious of the crossed feet's weight. And the
defenseless human thing sleeps as sound as if

incised with hard wrinkles, embossed with wide ears,
invincibly tusked, made safe by magic hairs!
As if, as if, it is all ifs; we are at
much unease. But magic's masterpiece is theirs –

Houdini's serenity quelling his fears.
Elephant-ear-witnesses-to-be of hymns
and glorias, these ministrants all gray or
gray with white on legs or trunk, are a pilgrims'

pattern of revery not reverence – a
religious procession without any priests,
the centuries-old carefullest unrehearsed
play. Blessed by Buddha's Tooth, the obedient beasts

themselves as toothed temples blessing the street, see
the white elephant carry the cushion that
carries the casket that carries the Tooth.
Amenable to what, matched with him, are gnat

trustees, he does not step on them as the white-
canopied blue-cushioned Tooth is augustly
and slowly returned to the shrine. Though white is
the color of worship and of mourning, he

is not here to worship and he is too wise
to mourn – a life prisoner but reconciled.
With trunk tucked up compactly – the elephant's
sign of defeat – he resisted, but is the child

of reason now. His straight trunk seems to say: when
what we hoped for came to nothing, we revived.
As loss could not ever alter Socrates'
tranquillity, equanimity's contrived

by the elephant. With the Socrates of
animals as with Sophocles the Bee, on whose
tombstone a hive was incised, sweetness tinctures
his gravity. His held-up fore-leg for use

as a stair, to be climbed or descended with
the aid of his ear, expounds the brotherhood
of creatures to man the encroacher, by the
small word with the dot, meaning know – the verb búd.

These knowers 'arouse the feeling that they are
allied to man' and can change roles with their trustees.
Hardship makes the soldier; then teachableness
makes him the philosopher – as Socrates,

prudently testing the suspicious thing, knew
the wisest is he who's not sure that he knows.
Who rides on a tiger can never dismount;
asleep on an elephant, that is repose.

MARIANNE MOORE

Engraved on the Collar of a Dog
which I Gave to His Royal Highness

[Frederick, Prince of Wales, father of George III]

I am his Highness' dog at Kew;
Pray tell me, sir, whose dog are you?

ALEXANDER POPE

Epigraph to *Pagett, M.P.*

The toad beneath the harrow knows
Exactly where each tooth-point goes;
The butterfly upon the road
Preaches contentment to that toad.

RUDYARD KIPLING

Epitaph on a Hare

Here lies, whom hound did ne'er pursue,
　　Nor swifter greyhound follow,
Whose foot ne'er tainted morning dew,
　　Nor ear heard huntsman's hallo',

Old Tiney, surliest of his kind,
　　Who, nursed with tender care,
And to domestic bounds confined,
　　Was still a wild jack-hare.

Though duly from my hand he took
　　His pittance every night,
He did it with a jealous look,
　　And, when he could, would bite.

His diet was of wheaten bread,
  And milk, and oats, and straw,
Thistles, or lettuces instead,
  With sand to scour his maw.

On twigs of hawthorn he regaled,
  On pippins' russet peel;
And, when his juicy salads failed,
  Sliced carrot pleased him well.

A Turkey carpet was his lawn,
  Whereon he loved to bound,
To skip and gambol like a fawn,
  And swing his rump around.

His frisking was at evening hours,
  For then he lost his fear;
But most before approaching showers,
  Or when a storm drew near.

Eight years and five round-rolling moons
  He thus saw steal away,
Dozing out all his idle noons,
  And every night at play.

I kept him for his humor's sake,
  For he would oft beguile
My heart of thoughts that made it ache,
  And force me to a smile.

But now, beneath this walnut-shade
  He finds his long, last home,
And waits in snug concealment laid,
  Till gentler Puss shall come.

He, still more agéd, feels the shocks
  From which no care can save,
And, partner once of Tiney's box,
  Must soon partake his grave.

WILLIAM COWPER

from Essay on Man

What would this man? Now upward will he soar,
And little less than angel, would be more;
Now looking downwards, just as grieved appears,
To want the strength of bulls, the fur of bears.
Made for his use all creatures if he call,
Say what their use, had he the powers of all?
Nature to these, without profusion, kind,
The proper organs, proper powers assign'd;
Each seeming what compensated of course,
Here with degrees of swiftness, there of force;
All in exact proportion to the state;
Nothing to add, and nothing to abate.
Each beast, each insect, happy in its own:
Is Heaven unkind to man, and man alone?
Shall he alone, whom rational we call,
Be pleased with nothing, if not blest with all?
   The bliss of man (could pride that blessing find)
Is not to act or think beyond mankind;
No powers of body or of soul to share,
But what his Nature and his state can bear.
Why has not man a microscopic eye?
For this plain reason, man is not a fly.
Say what the use, were finer optics given,
To inspect a mite, not comprehend the heaven?
Or touch, if trembling alive all o'er,
To smart and agonise at every pore?
Or quick effluvia darting through the brain,
Die of a rose in aromatic pain?
If Nature thunder'd in his opening ears,
And stunn'd him with the music of the spheres,
How would he wish that Heaven had left him still
The whisp'ring zephyr, and the purling rill?
Who finds not Providence all good and wise,
Alike in what it gives and what denies?
   Far as creation's ample range extends,
The scale of sensual, mental powers ascends:
Mark how it mounts to man's imperial race,

From the green myriads in the peopled grass:
What modes of sight betwixt each wide extreme,
The mole's dim curtain, and the lynx's beam:
Of smell, the headlong lioness between,
And hound sagacious on the tainted green:
Of hearing, from the life that fills the flood,
To that which warbles through the vernal wood?
The spider's touch, how exquisitely fine!
Feels at each thread, and lives along the line:
In the nice bee, what sense so subtly true
From poisonous herbs extract the healing dew?
How instinct varies in the grov'ling swine,
Compared, half-reasoning elephant, with thine!
'Twixt that, and reason, what a nice barrier?
For ever separate, yet for ever near!
Remembrance and reflection, how allied;
What thin partitions sense from thought divide;
And middle natures, how they long to join,
Yet never pass the insuperable line!
Without this just gradation could they be
Subjected, these to those, or all to thee?
The powers of all subdued by thee alone,
Is not thy reason all these powers in one?

ALEXANDER POPE

The Fall of Rome

For Cyril Connolly

The piers are pummelled by the waves;
In a lonely field the rain
Lashes an abandoned train;
Outlaws fill the mountain caves.

Fantastic grow the evening gowns;
Agents of the Fisc pursue
Absconding tax-defaulters through
The sewers of provincial towns.

Private rites of magic send
The temple prostitutes to sleep;
All the literati keep
An imaginary friend.

Cerebrotonic Cato may
Extoll the Ancient Disciplines,
But the muscle-bound Marines
Mutiny for food and pay.

Caesar's double-bed is warm
As an unimportant clerk
Writes *I DO NOT LIKE MY WORK*
On a pink official form.

Unendowed with wealth or pity,
Little birds with scarlet legs,
Sitting on their speckled eggs,
Eye each flu-infected city.

Altogether elsewhere, vast
Herds of reindeer move across
Miles and miles of golden moss,
Silently and very fast.

W. H. AUDEN

The Fallow Deer at the Lonely House

One without looks in to-night
    Through the curtain-chink
From the sheet of glistening white;
One without looks in to-night
    As we sit and think
    By the fender-brink.

We do not discern those eyes
    Watching in the snow;

Lit by lamps of rosy dyes
We do not discern those eyes
   Wondering, aglow,
   Fourfooted, tiptoe.

    THOMAS HARDY

February 17th

A lamb could not get born. Ice wind
Out of a downpour dishclout sunrise. The mother
Lay on the mudded slope. Harried, she got up
And the blackish lump bobbed at her back-end
Under her tail. After some hard galloping,
Some manoeuvring, much flapping of the backward
Lump head of the lamb looking out,
I caught her with a rope. Laid her, head uphill
And examined the lamb. A blood-ball swollen
Tight in its black felt, its mouth gap
Squashed crooked, tongue stuck out, black-purple,
Strangled by its mother. I felt inside,
Past the noose of mother-flesh, into the slippery
Muscled tunnel, fingering for a hoof,
Right back to the port-hole of the pelvis.
But there was no hoof. He had stuck his head out too early
And his feet could not follow. He should have
Felt his way, tip-toe, his toes
Tucked up under his nose
For a safe landing. So I kneeled wrestling
With her groans. No hand could squeeze past
The lamb's neck into her interior
To hook a knee. I roped that baby head
And hauled till she cried out and tried
To get up and I saw it was useless. I went
Two miles for the injection and a razor.
Sliced the lamb's throat-strings, levered with a knife
Between the vertebrae and brought the head off
To stare at its mother, its pipes sitting in the mud

With all earth for a body. Then pushed
The neck-stump right back in, and as I pushed
She pushed. She pushed crying and I pushed gasping.
And the strength
Of the birth push and the push of my thumb
Against that wobbly vertebra were deadlock,
A to-fro futility. Till I forced
A hand past and got a knee. Then like
Pulling myself to the ceiling with one finger
Hooked in a loop, timing my effort
To her birth push groans, I pulled against
The corpse that would not come. Till it came.
And after it the long, sudden, yolk-yellow
Parcel of life
In a smoking slither of oils and soups and syrups –
And the body lay born; beside the hacked-off head.

TED HUGHES

The Female of the Species

When the Himalayan peasant meets the he-bear in his pride,
He shouts to scare the monster, who will often turn aside.
But the she-bear thus accosted rends the peasant tooth and nail.
For the female of the species is more deadly than the male.

When Nag the basking cobra hears the careless foot of man,
He will sometimes wriggle sideways and avoid it if he can.
But his mate makes no such motion where she camps beside the trail.
For the female of the species is more deadly than the male.

When the early Jesuit fathers preached to Hurons and Choctaws,
They prayed to be delivered from the vengeance of the squaws.
'Twas the women, not the warriors, turned those stark enthusiasts pale.
For the female of the species is more deadly than the male.

Man's timid heart is bursting with the things he must not say,
For the Woman that God gave him isn't his to give away;
But when hunter meets with husband, each confirms the other's tale –

The female of the species is more deadly than the male.

Man, a bear in most relations – worm and savage otherwise, –
Man propounds negotiations, Man accepts the compromise.
Very rarely will he squarely push the logic of a fact
To its ultimate conclusion in unmitigated act.

Fear, or foolishness, impels him, ere he lay the wicked low,
To concede some form of trial even to his fiercest foe.
Mirth obscene diverts his anger – Doubt and Pity oft perplex
Him in dealing with an issue – to the scandal of The Sex!

But the Woman that God gave him, every fibre of her frame
Proves her launched for one sole issue, armed and engined for the
    same;
And to serve that single issue, lest the generations fail,
The female of the species must be deadlier than the male.

She who faces Death by torture for each life beneath her breast
May not deal in doubt or pity – must not swerve for fact or jest.
These be purely male diversions – not in these her honour dwells.
She the Other Law we live by, is that Law and nothing else.

She can bring no more to living than the powers that make her great
As the Mother of the Infant and the Mistress of the Mate.
And when Babe and Man are lacking and she strides unclaimed to
    claim
Her right as femme (and baron), her equipment is the same.

She is wedded to convictions – in default of grosser ties;
Her contentions are her children, Heaven help him who denies! –
He will meet no suave discussion, but the instant, white-hot, wild,
Wakened female of the species warring as for spouse and child.

Unprovoked and awful charges – even so the she-bear fights,
Speech that drips, corrodes, and poisons – even so the cobra bites,
Scientific vivisection of one nerve till it is raw
And the victim writhes in anguish – like the Jesuit with the squaw!

So it comes that Man, the coward, when he gathers to confer
With his fellow-braves in council, dare not leave a place for her
Where, at war with Life and Conscience, he uplifts his erring hands
To some God of Abstract Justice – which no woman understands.

And Man knows it! Knows, moreover, that the Woman that God gave
    him
Must command but may not govern – shall enthral but not enslave
    him.
And *She* knows, because She warns him, and Her instincts never fail,
That the Female of Her Species is more deadly than the Male.

RUDYARD KIPLING

Fetching Cows

The black one, last as usual, swings her head
And coils a black tongue round a grass-tuft. I
Watch her soft weight come down, her split feet spread.

In front, the others swing and slouch; they roll
Their great Greek eyes and breathe out milky gusts
From muzzles black and shiny as wet coal.

The collie trots, bored, at my heels, then plops
Into the ditch. The sea makes a tired sound
That's always stopping though it never stops.

A haycart squats prickeared against the sky.
Hay breath and milk breath. Far out in the West
The wrecked sun founders though its colours fly.

The collie's bored. There's nothing to control . . .
The black cow is two native carriers
Bringing its belly home, slung from a pole.

NORMAN MACCAIG

Fireflies in the Garden

Here come real stars to fill the upper skies,
And here on earth come emulating flies
That, though they never equal stars in size

(And they were never really stars at heart),
Achieve at times a very starlike start.
Only, of course, they can't sustain the part.

ROBERT FROST

The Fish

I caught a tremendous fish
and held him beside the boat
half out of water, with my hook
fast in a corner of his mouth.
He didn't fight.
He hadn't fought at all.
He hung a grunting weight,
battered and venerable
and homely. Here and there
his brown skin hung in strips
like ancient wallpaper,
and its pattern of darker brown
was like wallpaper:
shapes like full-blown roses
stained and lost through age.
He was speckled with barnacles,
fine rosettes of lime,
and infested
with tiny white sea-lice,
and underneath two or three
rags of green weed hung down.
While his gills were breathing in
the terrible oxygen
– the frightening gills,
fresh and crisp with blood,
that can cut so badly –
I thought of the coarse white flesh
packed in like feathers,
the big bones and the little bones,
the dramatic reds and blacks

of his shiny entrails,
and the pink swim-bladder
like a big peony.
I looked into his eyes
which were far larger than mine
but shallower, and yellowed,
the irises backed and packed
with tarnished tinfoil
seen through the lenses
of old scratched isinglass.
They shifted a little, but not
to return my stare.
– It was more like the tipping
of an object toward the light.
I admired his sullen face,
the mechanism of his jaw,
and then I saw
that from his lower lip
– if you could call it a lip –
grim, wet, and weaponlike,
hung five old pieces of fish-line,
or four and a wire leader
with the swivel still attached,
with all their five big hooks
grown firmly in his mouth.
A green line, frayed at the end
where he broke it, two heavier lines,
and a fine black thread
still crimped from the strain and snap
when it broke and he got away.
Like medals with their ribbons
frayed and wavering,
a five-haired beard of wisdom
trailing from his aching jaw.
I stared and stared
and victory filled up
the little rented boat,
from the pool of bilge
where oil had spread a rainbow
around the rusted engine

to the bailer rusted orange,
the sun-cracked thwarts,
the oarlocks on their strings,
the gunnels – until everything
was rainbow, rainbow, rainbow!
And I let the fish go.

ELIZABETH BISHOP

The Fish

wade
through black jade.
   Of the crow-blue mussel-shells, one keeps
   adjusting the ash-heaps;
      opening and shutting itself like

an
injured fan.
   The barnacles which encrust the side
   of the wave, cannot hide
      there for the submerged shafts of the

sun,
split like spun
   glass, move themselves with spotlight swiftness
   into the crevices –
      in and out, illuminating

the
turquoise sea
   of bodies. The water drives a wedge
   of iron through the iron edge
      of the cliff; whereupon the stars,

pink
rice-grains, ink-
   bespattered jelly-fish, crabs like green
   lilies, and submarine
      toadstools, slide each on the other.

All
external
    marks of abuse are present on this
    defiant edifice –
        all the physical features of

ac-
cident – lack
    of cornice, dynamite grooves, burns, and
    hatchet strokes, these things stand
        out on it; the chasm-side is

dead.
Repeated
    evidence has proved that it can live
    on what can not revive
        its youth. The sea grows old in it.

MARIANNE MOORE

The Flea

Mark but this flea, and mark in this,
How little that which thou deny'st me is;
It suck'd me first, and now sucks thee,
And in this flea, our two bloods mingled be;
Thou know'st that this cannot be said
A sin, nor shame, nor loss of maidenhead,
    Yet this enjoys before it woo,
    And pamper'd swells with one blood made of two,
    And this, alas, is more than we would do.

Oh stay, three lives in one flea spare,
Where we almost, yea more than married are.
This flea is you and I, and this
Our marriage bed, and marriage temple is;
Though parents grudge, and you, we're met,
And cloister'd in these living walls of jet.

Though use make you apt to kill me,
Let not to that, self-murder added be,
And sacrilege, three sins in killing three.

Cruel and sudden, hast thou since
Purpled thy nail, in blood of innocence?
Wherein could this flea guilty be,
Except in that drop which it suck'd from thee?
Yet thou triumph'st, and say'st that thou
Find'st not thyself, nor me, the weaker now;
'Tis true, then learn how false, fears be;
Just so much honor, when thou yield'st to me,
Will waste, as this flea's death took life from thee.

JOHN DONNE

The Fly

Little Fly
Thy summers play,
My thoughtless hand
Has brush'd away.

Am not I
A fly like thee?
Or art not thou
A man like me?

For I dance
And drink & sing:
Till some blind hand
Shall brush my wing.

If thought is life
And strength & breath:
And the want
Of thought is death;

Then am I
A happy fly,
If I live,
Or if I die.

WILLIAM BLAKE

The Fly

She sat on a willow-trunk
watching
part of the battle of Crécy,
the shouts,
the gasps,
the groans,
the tramping and the tumbling.

During the fourteenth charge
of the French cavalry
she mated
with a brown-eyed male fly
from Vadincourt.

She rubbed her legs together
as she sat on a disembowelled horse
meditating
on the immortality of flies.

With relief she alighted
on the blue tongue
of the Duke of Clervaux.

When silence settled
and only the whisper of decay
softly circled the bodies

and only
a few arms and legs
still twitched jerkily under the trees,

she began to lay her eggs

on the single eye
of Johann Uhr,
the Royal Armourer.

And thus it was
that she was eaten by a swift
fleeing
from the fires of Estrées.

MIROSLAV HOLUB
Translated from the Czech by George Theiner

A Fly about a Glasse of Burnt Claret

Forbear this liquid Fire, *Fly*,
It is more fatal than the dry,
That singly, but embracing, wounds,
And this at once, both burns and drowns.

The Salamander that in heat
And flames doth cool his monstrous sweat;
Whose fan a glowing cake, is said,
Of this red furnace is afraid.

Viewing the Ruby-christal shine,
Thou tak'st it for Heaven-Christalline;
Anon thou wilt be taught to groan,
'Tis an ascended *Acheron*.

A Snowball heart in it let fall,
And take it out a Fire-ball:
An Icy breast in it betray'd
Breaks a destructive wild Granade.

'Tis, this, makes *Venus* Altars shine,
This kindles frosty *Hymen's* Pine;
When the Boy grows old in his desires,
This *Flambeau* doth new light his fires.

'Though the cold *Hermit* ever wail,
Whose sighs do freeze, and tears drop hail,
Once having passed this, will ne'r
Another flaming purging fear.

The *Vestal* drinking this doth burn,
Now more than in her fun'ral Urn;
Her fires, that with the Sun kept race,
Are now extinguish'd by her Face.

The *Chymist*, that himself doth still,
Let him but tast this *Limbecks* bill,
And prove this sublimated Bowl,
He'l swear it will calcine a Soul.

Noble and brave! now thou dost know,
The false prepared decks below,
Dost thou the fatal liquor sup,
One drop alas! thy Barque blowes up.

What airy Country hast to save,
Whose plagues thou'lt bury in thy grave?
For even now thou seemst to us
On this Gulphs brink a *Curtius*.

And now th' art faln (magnanimous *Fly*)
In, where thine Ocean doth fry,
Like the Sun's son who blush'd the flood,
To a complexion of blood.

Yet see! my glad Auricular
Redeems thee (though dissolv'd) a Star,
Flaggy thy Wings, and scorch'd thy Thighs,
Thou ly'st a double Sacrifice.

And now my warming, cooling, breath,
Shall a new life afford in Death;
See! in the Hospital of my hand
Already cur'd, thou fierce do'st stand.

Burnt Insect! dost thou reaspire
The moist-hot-glasse, and liquid fire?
I see! 'tis such a pleasing pain,
Thou would'st be scorch'd, and drown'd again.

RICHARD LOVELACE

Foweles in the Frith

Foweles in the frith,
The fisses in the flod,
And I mon waxe wod:
Mulch sorw I walke with
For beste of bon and blod.

ANONYMOUS

A Frog's Fate

Contemptuous of his home beyond
The village and the village-pond,
A large-souled Frog who spurned each byeway
Hopped along the imperial highway.

Nor grunting pig nor barking dog
Could disconcert so great a Frog.
The morning dew was lingering yet,
His sides to cool, his tongue to wet:
The night-dew, when the night should come,
A travelled Frog would send him home.

Not so, alas! The wayside grass
Sees him no more: not so, alas!
A broad-wheeled waggon unawares
Ran him down, his joys, his cares.
From dying choke one feeble croak
The Frog's perpetual silence broke: –

'Ye buoyant Frogs, ye great and small,
Even I am mortal after all!
My road to fame turns out a wry way;
I perish on the hideous highway;
Oh for my old familiar byeway!'

The choking Frog sobbed and was gone;
The Waggoner strode whistling on.
Unconscious of the carnage done,
Whistling that Waggoner strode on –
Whistling (it may have happened so)
'A froggy would a-wooing go.'
A hypothetic frog trolled he,
Obtuse to a reality.

O rich and poor, O great and small,
Such oversights beset us all.
The mangled Frog abides incog,
The uninteresting actual frog:
The hypothetic frog alone
Is the one frog we dwell upon.

CHRISTINA ROSSETTI

'From Paumanok starting I fly like a bird'

From Paumanok starting I fly like a bird,
Around and around to soar to sing the idea of all,
To the north betaking myself to sing there arctic songs,
To Kanada till I absorb Kanada in myself, to Michigan then,
To Wisconsin, Iowa, Minnesota, to sing their songs, (they are
    inimitable)
Then to Ohio and Indiana to sing theirs, to Missouri and Kansas and
    Arkansas to sing theirs,
To Tennessee and Kentucky, to the Carolinas and Georgia to sing
    theirs,
To Texas and so along up toward California, to roam accepted
    everywhere,

To sing first, (to the tap of the war-drum if need be,)
The idea of all, of the Western world one and inseparable,
And then the song of each member of these States.

WALT WHITMAN

Glazunoviana

The man with the red hat
And the polar bear, is he here too?
The window giving on shade,
Is that here too?
And all the little helps,
My initials in the sky,
The hay of an arctic summer night?

The bear
Drops dead in sight of the window.
Lovely tribes have just moved to the north.
In the flickering evening the martins grow denser.
Rivers of wings surround us and vast tribulation.

JOHN ASHBERY

The Goose and the Gander

O the goose and the gander walk'd over the green,
O the goose she went barefoot for fear of being seen,
For fear of being seen, boys, for fear of being seen,
And the goose she went barefoot for fear of being seen.

I had a black hen and she had a white foot,
And she laid an egg in a willow tree root,
In a willow tree root, in a willow tree root,
And she laid a white egg in a willow tree root.

ANONYMOUS

Goose to Donkey

My big friend, I bow help;
I bow, Get up, big friend:
let me land-swim again beside your clicky feet,
don't sleep flat with dried wet in your holes.

LES MURRAY

Goosey Gander

Goosey, goosey gander,
  Whither shall I wander?
Upstairs and downstairs
  And in my lady's chamber.
There I met an old man
  Who would not say his prayers,
I took him by the left leg
  And threw him down the stairs.

ANONYMOUS

Grand Chorus of Birds

(after Aristophanes)

Come on then, ye dwellers by nature in darkness, and like to the leaves'
  generations,
That are little of might, that are moulded of mire, unenduring and
  shadowlike nations,
Poor plumeless ephemerals, comfortless mortals, as visions of creatures
  fast fleeing,
Lift up your mind unto us that are deathless, and dateless the date of
  our being:
Us, children of heaven, us, ageless for aye, us, all of whose thoughts
  are eternal;

That ye may from henceforth, having heard of us all things aright as to matters supernal,

Of the being of birds and beginning of gods, and of streams, and the dark beyond reaching,

Truthfully knowing aright, in my name bid Prodicus pack with his preaching.

It was Chaos and Night at the first, and the blackness of darkness, and hell's broad border,

Earth was not, nor air, neither heaven; when in depths of the womb of the dark without order

First thing first-born of the black-plumed Night was a wind-egg hatched in her bosom,

Whence timely with seasons revolving again sweet Love burst out as a blossom,

Gold wings glittering forth of his back, like whirlwinds gustily turning,

He, after his wedlock with Chaos, whose wings are of darkness, in hell broad-burning,

For his nestlings begat him the race of us first, and upraised us to light new-lighted.

And before this was not the race of the gods, until all things by Love were united;

And of kind united with kind in communion of nature the sky and the sea are

Brought forth, and the earth, and the race of the gods everlasting and blest. So that we are

Far away the most ancient of all things blest. And that we are of Love's generation

There are manifest manifold signs. We have wings, and with us have the Loves habitation;

And manifold fair young folk that forswore love once, ere the bloom of them ended,

Have the men that pursued and desired them subdued, by the help of us only befriended,

With such baits as a quail, a flamingo, a goose, or a cock's comb staring and splendid.

All best good things that befall men come from us birds, as is plain to all reason:

For first we proclaim and make known to them spring, and the winter and autumn in season;

Bid sow, when the crane starts clanging for Afric, in shrill-voiced
    emigrant number,
And calls to the pilot to hang up his rudder again for the season, and
    slumber;
And then weave cloak for Orestes the thief, lest he strip men of theirs
    if it freezes.
And again thereafter the kite reappearing announces a change in the
    breezes,
And that here is the season for shearing your sheep of their spring
    wool. Then does the swallow
Give you notice to sell your greatcoat, and provide something light for
    the heat that's to follow.
Thus are we as Ammon or Delphi unto you, Dodona, nay, Phoebus
    Apollo.
For, as first ye come all to get auguries of birds, even such is in all
    things your carriage,
Be the matter a matter of trade, or of earning your bread, or of any
    one's marriage.
And all things ye lay to the charge of a bird that belong to discerning
    prediction:
Winged fame is a bird, as you reckon: you sneeze, and the sign's as a
    bird for conviction:
All tokens are 'birds' with you – sounds too, and lackeys, and donkeys.
    Then must it not follow
That we ARE to you all as the manifest godhead that speaks in prophetic
    Apollo?

ALGERNON CHARLES SWINBURNE

The Grasshopper

To my noble friend, Mr Charles Cotton

O thou that swing'st upon the waving hair
    Of some well-filléd oaten beard,
Drunk every night with a delicious tear
    Dropped thee from heaven, where now th' art reared;

The joys of earth and air are thine entire,
  That with thy feet and wings dost hop and fly;
And, when thy poppy works, thou dost retire
  To thy carved acorn-bed to lie.

Up with the day, the sun thou welcom'st then,
  Sport'st in the gilt plats of his beams,
And all these merry days mak'st merry men,
  Thyself, and melancholy streams.

But ah, the sickle! Golden ears are cropped;
  Ceres and Bacchus bid good night;
Sharp, frosty fingers all your flowers have topped,
  And what scythes spared, winds shave off quite.

Poor verdant fool, and now green ice! thy joys,
  Large and as lasting as thy perch of grass,
Bid us lay in 'gainst winter rain, and poise
  Their floods with an o'erflowing glass.

Thou best of men and friends! we will create
  A genuine summer in each other's breast,
And spite of this cold time and frozen fate,
  Thaw us a warm seat to our rest.

Our sacred hearths shall burn eternally,
  As vestal flames; the North Wind, he
Shall strike his frost-stretched wings, dissolve, and fly
  This Etna in epitome.

Dropping December shall come weeping in,
  Bewail th' usurping of his reign:
But when in showers of old Greek we begin,
  Shall cry he hath his crown again!

Night, as clear Hesper, shall our tapers whip
  From the light casements where we play,
And the dark hag from her black mantle strip,
  And stick there everlasting day.

Thus richer than untempted kings are we,
    That, asking nothing, nothing need:
Though lord of all what seas embrace, yet he
    That wants himself is poor indeed.

RICHARD LOVELACE

The Grasshopper and the Ant

Grasshopper, having sung her song
    All summer long,
Was sadly unprovided-for
When the cold winds began to roar:
Not one least bite of grub or fly
Had she remembered to put by.
Therefore she hastened to descant
On famine, to her neighbor Ant,
Begging the loan of a few grains
Of wheat to ease her hunger-pains
Until the winter should be gone.
'You shall be paid,' said she, 'upon
My honor as an animal,
Both interest and principal.'
The Ant was not disposed to lend;
That liberal vice was not for her.
'What did you do all summer, friend?'
She asked the would-be borrower.
'So please your worship,' answered she,
'I sang and sang both night and day.'
'You sang? Indeed, that pleases me.
Then dance the winter-time away.'

JEAN DE LA FONTAINE
Translated from the French by Richard Wilbur

The Great Horned Owl

One morning the Grand Seigneur
Is so good as to appear.
He sits in a scrawny little tree
In my backyard.

When I say his name aloud,
He turns his head
And looks at me
In utter disbelief.

I show him my belt,
How I had to
Tighten it lately
To the final hole.

He ruffles his feathers,
Studies the empty woodshed,
The old red Chevy on blocks.
Alas! He's got to be going.

CHARLES SIMIC

The Green Linnet

Beneath these fruit-tree boughs that shed
Their snow-white blossoms on my head,
With brightest sunshine round me spread
    Of spring's unclouded weather,
In this sequestered nook how sweet
To sit upon my orchard-seat!
And birds and flowers once more to greet,
    My last year's friends together.

One have I marked, the happiest guest
In all this covert of the blest:
Hail to Thee, far above the rest
    In joy of voice and pinion!
Thou, Linnet! in thy green array,

And thought of China and of Greece,
Of Alexander in his tent;
Of Montaigne in his tower,
Of Saint Theresa in her wild lament.

RICHARD EBERHART

The Groundlark

Close where the milking maidens pass
In roots and twitches drest
Within a little bunch of grass
A groundlark made her nest
The maiden touched her with her gown
And often frit her out
And looked and set her buckets down
But never found it out
The eggs were large and spotted round
And dark as is the fallow ground
The schoolboy kicked the grass in play
But danger never guest
And when they came to mow the hay
They found an empty nest

JOHN CLARE

Hark! Hark! the Lark

Hark, hark! the lark at heaven's gate sings,
    And Phoebus 'gins arise,
His steeds to water at those springs
    On chaliced flowers that lies;
And winking Mary-buds begin
    To ope their golden eyes:

With every thing that pretty is,
   My lady sweet, arise:
   Arise, arise!

WILLIAM SHAKESPEARE

The Hart Loves the High Wood

The Hart loves the high wood,
   the Hare loves the hill,
The Knight loves his bright sword,
   the Churl loves his bill.

ANONYMOUS

The Heaven of Animals

Here they are. The soft eyes open.
If they have lived in a wood
It is a wood.
If they have lived on plains
It is grass rolling
Under their feet forever.

Having no souls, they have come,
Anyway, beyond their knowing.
Their instincts wholly bloom
And they rise.
The soft eyes open.

To match them, the landscape flowers,
Outdoing, desperately
Outdoing what is required:
The richest wood,
The deepest field.

For some of these,
It could not be the place

It is, without blood.
These hunt, as they have done,
But with claws and teeth grown perfect,

More deadly than they can believe.
They stalk more silently,
And crouch on the limbs of trees,
And their descent
Upon the bright backs of their prey

May take years
In a sovereign floating of joy.
And those that are hunted
Know this as their life,
Their reward: to walk

Under such trees in full knowledge
Of what is in glory above them,
And to feel no fear,
But acceptance, compliance.
Fulfilling themselves without pain

At the cycle's center,
They tremble, they walk
Under the tree,
They fall, they are torn,
They rise, they walk again.

JAMES DICKEY

The Heavy Bear who Goes with Me

'the withness of the body'

The heavy bear who goes with me,
A manifold honey to smear his face,
Clumsy and lumbering here and there,
The central ton of every place,
The hungry beating brutish one
In love with candy, anger, and sleep,

Crazy factotum, dishevelling all,
Climbs the building, kicks the football,
Boxes his brother in the hate-ridden city.

Breathing at my side, that heavy animal,
That heavy bear who sleeps with me,
Howls in his sleep for a world of sugar,
A sweetness intimate as the water's clasp,
Howls in his sleep because the tight-rope
Trembles and shows the darkness beneath.
– The strutting show-off is terrified,
Dressed in his dress-suit, bulging his pants,
Trembles to think that his quivering meat
Must finally wince to nothing at all.

That inescapable animal walks with me,
Has followed me since the black womb held,
Moves where I move, distorting my gesture,
A caricature, a swollen shadow,
A stupid clown of the spirit's motive,
Perplexes and affronts with his own darkness,
The secret life of belly and bone,
Opaque, too near, my private, yet unknown,
Stretches to embrace the very dear
With whom I would walk without him near,
Touches her grossly, although a word
Would bare my heart and make me clear,
Stumbles, flounders, and strives to be fed
Dragging me with him in his mouthing care,
Amid the hundred million of his kind,
The scrimmage of appetite everywhere.

DELMORE SCHWARTZ

The Hedgehog

The hedgehog hides beneath the rotten hedge
And makes a great round nest of grass and sedge
Or in a bush or in a hollow tree

And many often stoops and say they see
Him roll and fill his prickles full of crab[s]
And creep away and where the magpie dabs
His wing at muddy dyke in aged root
He makes a nest and fills it full of fruit
On the hedge bottom hunts for crabs and sloes
And whistles like a cricket as he goes
It rolls up like a ball a shapeless hog
When gipseys hunt it with their noisey dogs
Ive seen it in their camps they call it sweet
Though black and bitter and unsavoury meat

But they who hunt the fields for rotten meat
And wash in muddy dyke and call it sweet
And eat what dogs refuse where ere they dwell
Care little either for the taste or smell
They say they milk the cows and when they lye
Nibble their fleshy teats and make them dry
But they whove seen the small head like a hog
Rolled up to meet the savage of a dog
With mouth scarce big enough to hold a straw
Will neer believe what no one ever saw
But still they hunt the hedges all about
And shepherd dogs are trained to hunt them out
They hurl with savage force the stick and stone
And no one cares and still the strife goes on

JOHN CLARE

Hen

The hen is the best example of what living constantly with humans
leads to. She has completely lost the lightness and grace of a bird.
Her tail sticks up over her protruding rump like a too large hat in bad
taste. Her rare moments of ecstasy, when she stands on one leg and
glues up her round eyes with filmy eyelids, are stunningly disgusting.
And in addition, that parody of song, throat-slashed supplications
over a thing unutterably comic: a round, white, maculated egg.

The hen brings to mind certain poets.

ZBIGNIEW HERBERT
Translated from the Polish by Czesław Miłosz

Hickory, Dickory, Dock

Hickory, dickory, dock,
The mouse ran up the clock.
  The clock struck one,
  The mouse ran down,
Hickory, dickory, dock.

ANONYMOUS

The Hippopotamus

*Similiter et omnes revereantur Diaconos, ut mandatum Jesu Christi; et
Episcopum, ut Jesum Christum, existentem filium Patris; Presbyteros autem,
ut concilium Dei et conjunctionem Apostolorum. Sine his Ecclesia non vocatur;
de quibus suadeo vos sic habeo.*
  S. Ignatii Ad Trallianos

*And when this epistle is read among you, cause that it be read also in the
church of the Laodiceans.*

The broad-backed hippopotamus
Rests on his belly in the mud;
Although he seems so firm to us
He is merely flesh and blood.

  Flesh and blood is weak and frail,
Susceptible to nervous shock;
While the True Church can never fail
For it is based upon a rock.

The hippo's feeble steps may err
In compassing material ends,
While the True Church need never stir
To gather in its dividends.

The 'potamus can never reach
The mango on the mango-tree;
But fruits of pomegranate and peach
Refresh the Church from over sea.

At mating time the hippo's voice
Betrays inflexions hoarse and odd,
But every week we hear rejoice
The Church, at being one with God.

The hippopotamus's day
Is passed in sleep; at night he hunts;
God works in a mysterious way –
The Church can sleep and feed at once.

I saw the 'potamus take wing
Ascending from the damp savannas,
And quiring angels round him sing
The praise of God, in loud hosannas.

Blood of the Lamb shall wash him clean
And him shall heavenly arms enfold,
Among the saints he shall be seen
Performing on a harp of gold.

He shall be washed as white as snow,
By all the martyr'd virgins kist,
While the True Church remains below
Wrapt in the old miasmal mist.

T. S. ELIOT

'His Mansion in the Pool'

His Mansion in the Pool
The Frog forsakes –

He rises on a Log
And statements makes –
His Auditors two Worlds
Deducting me –
The Orator of April
Is hoarse Today –
His Mittens at his Feet
No Hand hath he –
His eloquence a Bubble
As Fame should be –
Applaud him to discover
To your chagrin
Demosthenes has vanished
In Waters Green –

EMILY DICKINSON

The Horse

Many times man's size, the horse has flared nostrils, round eyes under half-closed lids, pricked ears and a sinewy long neck.

The highest of man's domesticated animals, and truly meant to be his mount.

Man, a little lost on the elephant, is seen to his advantage on the horse, a throne truly to his measure.

We will not, I hope, abandon it?

He will not become a curiosity in the Zoo, or the Tiergarten?

... Already, in town, it is no more than a miserable makeshift automobile, the most miserable means of traction.

Ah, it is also – does man realise it? – something else entirely. It is nostrilled impatience.

The arms of the horse are flight, bite, and buck.

It seems he has a keen nose and ear and a very sensitive eye.

One of the finest homages we feel obliged to give, is to have to blinker him.

But wholly unarmed . . .
Whence the temptation to add one to him. One only. A horn.
Then the unicorn appears.

The horse, notoriously nervous, is a wind eater.
Highly strung, he clenches his jaws, holds his breath, then releases
it, making the walls of his nasal passages vibrate loudly.
That is why this noble animal, which feeds itself only on grass and
air, only produces straw brioches and fragrant and thunderous farts.
Fragrant thunderballs.

What am I saying, feeds on air? he gets drunk on it.
Swallows, snuffles, snorts it.

He rushes into it, shaking his mane, rears up his hind legs into it.
He would clearly like to take off.
The flight of clouds inspires, irritates him into emulation.
He imitates it: he tosses his mane, prances . . .
When the lightning of the whip smacks, the clouds gallop quicker
and the rain tramples the soil . . .

Break out of your paddock, impetuous, spirited chest-of-drawers
with round, well polished knobs!
Antique console, great and beautiful!
Polished ebony or mahogany.
Caress the décolleté of this chest and forthwith it takes on an absent-
minded look.
A snuffle at the lips, a feather plume at the rear, the key in the
nostrils' lock.
His skin quivers, impatiently enduring flies, his horseshoe hammers
the earth.
He lowers his head, leans his muzzle towards the ground, and guzzles
grass.
A stool is needed to look on the upper shelf.

A ticklish skin, as I was saying . . . but the impatience of his character
is so deep, that inside his body the parts of his hull disport like pebbles
in a torrent!
Viewed from the apse, the highest animal nave in the stable . . .

Great saint! great horse! beautiful bottom in the stable . . .

What is this splendid courtesan's rump that greets me, set on slim legs, on high heels?

Huge goose of golden eggs, so curiously shorn.

Ah, it is the odor of gold that hits me in the face!

Leather and dung mingled.

An omelette of straw, of earth, rum flavored from your urine, jetting from the crack under your flowing tail . . .

As sliding from the oven, on the pastry cook's tray, the brioches, the many-layered rum tarts of the stable.

Great saint, with your jewish eyes, sullen under the harness . . .

A sort of saint, a humble monk at orison, in the dusk.

Did I say monk? . . . No, ferried on his excremental litter, a pontiff! a pope displaying to all comers a splendid courtesan's bottom, open heart shaped, on nervous legs tapering to elegant high-heeled shoes.

WHY THIS CLICKING OF THE BIT?

THESE MUFFLED THUDS IN THE STALL?

WHAT'S HAPPENING IN THE HORSE BOX?

A PONTIFF AT PRAYER?

A SCHOOLBOY DETAINED?

GREAT SAINT! GREAT HORSE (HORSE OR HERO?) BEAUTIFUL BOTTOM IN THE STABLE,

WHY, SAINT MONK, DID YOU CLOTHE YOUR BUTTOCKS SO BOLDLY IN LEATHER?

— DISTURBED IN HIS MASS, HE TURNED TOWARDS US THOSE JEWISH EYES . . .

FRANCIS PONGE
Translated from the French by John Montague

The Horse

The horse moves
independently
without reference
to his load

He has eyes
like a woman and
turns them
about, throws

back his ears
and is generally
conscious of
the world. Yet

he pulls when
he must and
pulls well, blowing
fog from

his nostrils
like fumes from
the twin
exhausts of a car.

WILLIAM CARLOS WILLIAMS

The Horses

Barely a twelvemonth after
The seven days' war that put the world to sleep,
Late in the evening the strange horses came.
By then we had made our covenant with silence,
But in the first few days it was so still
We listened to our breathing and were afraid.
On the second day
The radios failed; we turned the knobs; no answer.
On the third day a warship passed us, heading north,
Dead bodies piled on the deck. On the sixth day
A plane plunged over us into the sea. Thereafter
Nothing. The radios dumb;
And still they stand in corners of our kitchens,
And stand, perhaps, turned on, in a million rooms
All over the world. But now if they should speak,

If on a sudden they should speak again,
If on the stroke of noon a voice should speak,
We would not listen, we would not let it bring
That old bad world that swallowed its children quick
At one great gulp. We would not have it again.
Sometimes we think of the nations lying asleep,
Curled blindly in impenetrable sorrow,
And then the thought confounds us with its strangeness.
The tractors lie about our fields; at evening
They look like dank sea-monsters couched and waiting.
We leave them where they are and let them rust:
'They'll moulder away and be like other loam'.
We make our oxen drag our rusty ploughs,
Long laid aside. We have gone back
Far past our fathers' land.

                              And then, that evening
Late in the summer the strange horses came.
We heard a distant tapping on the road,
A deepening drumming; it stopped, went on again
And at the corner changed to hollow thunder.
We saw the heads
Like a wild wave charging and were afraid.
We had sold our horses in our fathers' time
To buy new tractors. Now they were strange to us
As fabulous steeds set on an ancient shield
Or illustrations in a book of knights.
We did not dare go near them. Yet they waited,
Stubborn and shy, as if they had been sent
By an old command to find our whereabouts
And that long-lost archaic companionship.
In the first moment we had never a thought
That they were creatures to be owned and used.
Among them were some half-a-dozen colts
Dropped in some wilderness of the broken world,
Yet new as if they had come from their own Eden.
Since then they have pulled our ploughs and borne our loads,
But that free servitude still can pierce our hearts.
Our life is changed; their coming our beginning.

   EDWIN MUIR

How They Brought the Good News from Ghent to Aix

I sprang to the stirrup, and Joris, and he;
I galloped, Dirck galloped, we galloped all three;
'Good speed!' cried the watch, as the gatebolts undrew;
'Speed!' echoed the wall to us galloping through;
Behind shut the postern, the lights sank to rest,
And into the midnight we galloped abreast.

Not a word to each other; we kept the great pace
Neck by neck, stride by stride, never changing our place;
I turned in my saddle and made its girths tight,
Then shortened each stirrup, and set the pique right,
Rebuckled the cheek-strap, chained slacker the bit,
Nor galloped less steadily Roland a whit.

'Twas moonset at starting; but while we drew near
Lokeren, the cocks crew and twilight dawned clear;
At Boom, a great yellow star came out to see;
At Düffeld, 'twas morning as plain as could be;
And from Mecheln church-steeple we heard the half-chime,
So, Joris broke silence with, 'Yet there is time!'

At Aershot, up leaped of a sudden the sun,
And against him the cattle stood black every one,
To stare thro' the mist at us galloping past,
And I saw my stout galloper Roland at last,
With resolute shoulders, each butting away
The haze, as some bluff river headland its spray:

And his low head and crest, just one sharp ear bent back
For my voice, and the other pricked out on his track;
And one eye's black intelligence, – ever that glance
O'er its white edge at me, his own master, askance!
And the thick heavy spume-flakes which aye and anon
His fierce lips shook upwards in galloping on.

By Hasselt, Dirck groaned; and cried Joris, 'Stay spur!
'Your Roos galloped bravely, the fault's not in her,
'We'll remember at Aix' – for one heard the quick wheeze

Of her chest, saw the stretched neck and staggering knees,
And sunk tail, and horrible heave of the flank,
As down on her haunches she shuddered and sank.

So, we were left galloping, Joris and I,
Past Looz and past Tongres, no cloud in the sky;
The broad sun above laughed a pitiless laugh,
'Neath our feet broke the brittle bright stubble like chaff;
Till over by Dalhem a dome-spire sprang white,
And 'Gallop,' gasped Joris, 'for Aix is in sight!'

'How they'll greet us!' – and all in a moment his roan
Rolled neck and croup over, lay dead as a stone;
And there was my Roland to bear the whole weight
Of the news which alone could save Aix from her fate,
With his nostrils like pits full of blood to the brim,
And with circles of red for his eye-sockets' rim.

Then I cast loose my buffcoat, each holster let fall,
Shook off both my jack-boots, let go belt and all,
Stood up in the stirrup, leaned, patted his ear,
Called my Roland his pet-name, my horse without peer;
Clapped my hands, laughed and sang, any noise, bad or good,
Till at length into Aix Roland galloped and stood.

And all I remember is – friends flocking round
As I sat with his head 'twixt my knees on the ground;
And no voice but was praising this Roland of mine,
As I poured down his throat our last measure of wine,
Which (the burgesses voted by common consent)
Was no more than his due who brought good news from Ghent.

ROBERT BROWNING

Humming-Bird

I can imagine, in some otherworld
Primeval-dumb, far back
In that most awful stillness, that only gasped and hummed,
Humming-birds raced down the avenues.

Before anything had a soul,
While life was a heave of Matter, half inanimate,
This little bit chipped off in brilliance
And went whizzing through the slow, vast, succulent stems.

I believe there were no flowers then,
In the world where the humming-bird flashed ahead of creation.
I believe he pierced the slow vegetable veins with his long beak.

Probably he was big
As mosses, and little lizards, they say, were once big.
Probably he was a jabbing, terrifying monster.

We look at him through the wrong end of the long telescope of Time,
Luckily for us.

D. H. LAWRENCE

Hunting Season

A shot: from crag to crag
    The tell-tale echoes trundle;
Some feathered he-or-she
    Is now a lifeless bundle
And, proud into a kitchen, some
Example of our tribe will come.

Down in the startled valley
    Two lovers break apart:
He hears the roaring oven
    Of a witch's heart;
Behind his murmurs of her name
She sees a marksman taking aim.

Reminded of the hour
    And that his chair is hard,
A deathless verse half done,
    One interrupted bard
Postpones his dying with a dish
Of several suffocated fish.

W. H. AUDEN

The Hyænas

After the burial-parties leave
   And the baffled kites have fled;
The wise hyænas come out at eve
   To take account of our dead.

How he died and why he died
   Troubles them not a whit.
They snout the bushes and stones aside
   And dig till they come to it.

They are only resolute they shall eat
   That they and their mates may thrive,
And they know that the dead are safer meat
   Than the weakest thing alive.

(For a goat may butt, and a worm may sting,
   And a child will sometimes stand;
But a poor dead soldier of the King
   Can never lift a hand.)

They whoop and halloo and scatter the dirt
   Until their tushes white
Take good hold in the army shirt,
   And tug the corpse to light,

And the pitiful face is shewn again
   For an instant ere they close;
But it is not discovered to living men –
   Only to God and to those

Who, being soulless, are free from shame,
   Whatever meat they may find.
Nor do they defile the dead man's name –
   That is reserved for his kind.

RUDYARD KIPLING

I Am a Horse

I travel in a train
that is overcrowded
in my compartment
each seat is taken by a woman
with a man sitting on her lap
the air is unbearably tropical
all the travellers have an enormous appetite
they eat without ceasing
suddenly the men
begin to whimper
and long for the maternal breast
they unbutton the women's blouses
and suck the fresh milk to their hearts' content
I alone do not suck
nor am I suckled
nobody sits on my lap
and I'm not on anyone's lap
because I am a horse
immense and upright I sit
with my hind-legs up on the train seat
and comfortably lean
on my fore-legs
I whinny a raucous neigh neigh neigh
on my breast glitter
the sex buttons of sex appeal
in neat little rows
like the glittering buttons on uniforms
oh summertime
oh wide wide world

HANS ARP
Translated from the French by Michael Benedikt

'I found an old textbook of animals'

I found an old textbook of animals,
Brehm, second volume, birds:
Description, in sweet language, of the lives
of crows, swallows and jays. A lot of mistakes
in Gothic printing, but a lot of love: 'Our
feathered friends,' 'emigrate to warmer
countries,' 'nest, dotted egg, soft plumage,
the nightingale,' 'prophets of spring,'
The Red-Breasted Robin.

Year of printing 1913, Germany
on the eve of the war which became
the eve of all my wars.

My good friend, who died in my arms and in his blood
in the sands of Ashdod, 1948, in June.

Oh, my friend,
red-breasted.

YEHUDA AMICHAI
Translated from the Hebrew by the author and Ted Hughes

I Have a Gentle Cock

I have a gentle cock,
    Croweth me day;
He doth me risen early
    My matins for to say.

I have a gentle cock,
    Comen he is of great;
His comb is of red coral,
    His tail is of jet.

I have a gentle cock,
   Comen he is of kind;
His comb is of red coral,
   His tail is of inde.

His legges be of azure,
   So gentle and so small;
His spurres are of silver white
   Into the wortewale.

His eyen are of crystal,
   Locked all in amber;
And every night he percheth him
   In my lady's chamber.

   ANONYMOUS

'I heard a Fly buzz'

I heard a Fly buzz – when I died –
The Stillness in the Room
Was like the Stillness in the Air –
Between the Heaves of Storm –

The Eyes around – had wrung them dry –
And Breaths were gathering firm
For that last Onset – when the King
Be witnessed – in the Room –

I willed my Keepsakes – Signed away
What portion of me be
Assignable – and then it was
There interposed a Fly –

With Blue – uncertain stumbling Buzz –
Between the light – and me –
And then the Windows failed – and then
I could not see to see –

   EMILY DICKINSON

from An Imitation of the Sixth Satire of the Second Book of Horace

Once on a time (so runs the Fable)
A Country Mouse, right hospitable,
Receiv'd a Town Mouse at his Board,
Just as a Farmer might a Lord.
A frugal Mouse upon the whole,
Yet lov'd his Friend, and had a Soul;
Knew what was handsome, and wou'd do't,
On just occasion, *coute qui coute*.
He brought him Bacon (nothing lean)
Pudding, that might have pleas'd a Dean;
Cheese, such as men in Suffolk make,
But wish'd it Stilton for his sake;
Yet to his Guest tho' no way sparing,
He eat himself the Rind and paring.
Our Courtier scarce could touch a bit,
But show'd his Breeding, and his Wit,
He did his best to seem to eat,
And cry'd, 'I vow you're mighty neat.
'But Lord, my Friend, this savage Scene!
'For God's sake, come, and live with Men:
'Consider, Mice, like Men, must die,
'Both small and great, both you and I:
'Then spend your life in Joy and Sport,
'(This doctrine, Friend, I learnt at Court.)'
   The veriest Hermit in the Nation
May yield, God knows, to strong Temptation.
Away they come, thro' thick and thin,
To a tall house near Lincoln's Inn:
('Twas on the night of a Debate,
When all their Lordships had sate late.)
   Behold the place, where if a Poet
Shin'd in Description, he might show it,
Tell how the Moon-beam trembling falls
And tips with silver all the walls:
Palladian walls, Venetian doors,
Grotesco roofs, and Stucco floors:

But let it (in a word) be said,
The Moon was up, and Men a-bed,
The Napkins white, the Carpet red:
The Guests withdrawn had left the Treat,
And down the Mice sat, *tête à tête.*

  Our Courtier walks from dish to dish,
Tastes for his Friend of Fowl and Fish;
Tells all their names, lays down the law,
'*Que ça est bon! Ah goutez ça!*
'That Jelly's rich, this Malmsey healing,
'Pray dip your Whiskers and your Tail in.'
Was ever such a happy Swain?
He stuffs and swills, and stuffs again.
'I'm quite asham'd – 'tis mighty rude
'To eat so much – but all's so good.
'I have a thousand thanks to give –
'My Lord alone knows how to live.'

  No sooner said, but from the Hall
Rush Chaplain, Butler, Dogs and all:
'A Rat, a Rat! clap to the door – '
The Cat comes bouncing on the floor.
O for the Heart of Homer's Mice,
Or Gods to save them in a trice!
(It was by Providence, they think,
For your damn'd Stucco has no chink)
'An't please your Honour,' quoth the Peasant,
'This same Dessert is not so pleasant:
'Give me again my hollow Tree!
'A Crust of Bread, and Liberty.'

  ALEXANDER POPE

In Come de Animuls Two by Two

In come de animuls two by two,
Hippopotamus and a kangaroo.
Dem bones gona rise agin.

Dem bones gona rise agin.
I knows it, indeed I knows it, brother.
I knows it, dem bones gona to rise agin.

In come de animuls three by three,
Two big cats and a bumble bee.
Dem bones gona rise agin

In come de animuls fo' by fo',
Two thru de winder and two thru de do'.
Dem bones gona rise agin.

In come de animuls five by five,
Almost dead and hardly alive.
Dem bones gona rise again.

In come de animuls six by six,
Three wid clubs and three wid sticks.
Dem bones gona rise agin.

In come de animuls seben by seben,
Fo' from Hell and de others from Heaven.
Dem bones gona rise agin.

In come de animuls eight by eight,
Four on time and de others late.
Dem bones gona rise agin.

In come de animuls nine by nine,
Four in front and five behind.
Dem bones gona rise agin.

In come de animuls ten by ten,
Five big roosters and five big hens.
Dem bones gona rise again.
Dem bones gona rise agin.
I knows it, indeed I knows it, brother.
I knows it, dem bones gona rise agin.

ANONYMOUS

from The Inferno (Canto I)

Midway on our life's journey, I found myself
  In dark woods, the right road lost. To tell
  About those woods is hard – so tangled and rough

And savage that thinking of it now, I feel
  The old fear stirring: death is hardly more bitter.
  And yet, to treat the good I found there as well

I'll tell what I saw, though how I came to enter
  I cannot well say, being so full of sleep
  Whatever moment it was I began to blunder

Off the true path. But when I came to stop
  Below a hill that marked one end of the valley
  That had pierced my heart with terror, I looked up

Toward the crest and saw its shoulders already
  Mantled in rays of that bright planet that shows
  The road to everyone, whatever our journey.

Then I could feel the terror begin to ease
  That churned in my heart's lake all through the night.
  As one still panting, ashore from dangerous seas,

Looks back at the deep he has escaped, my thought
  Returned, still fleeing, to regard that grim defile
  That never left any alive who stayed in it.

After I had rested my weary body awhile
  I started again across the wilderness,
  My left foot always lower on the hill,

And suddenly – a leopard, near the place
  The way grew steep: lithe, spotted, quick of foot.
  Blocking the path, she stayed before my face

And more than once she made me turn about
  To go back down. It was early morning still,
  The fair sun rising with the stars attending it

As when Divine Love set those beautiful
   Lights into motion at creation's dawn,
   And the time of day and season combined to fill

My heart with hope of that beast with festive skin –
   But not so much that the next sight wasn't fearful:
   A lion came at me, his head high as he ran,

Roaring with hunger so the air appeared to tremble.
   Then, a grim she-wolf – whose leanness seemed to compress
   All the world's cravings, that had made miserable

Such multitudes; she put such heaviness
   Into my spirit, I lost hope of the crest.
   Like someone eager to win, who tested by loss

Surrenders to gloom and weeps, so did that beast
   Make me feel, as harrying toward me at a lope
   She forced me back toward where the sun is lost.

While I was ruining myself back down to the deep,
   Someone appeared – one who seemed nearly to fade
   As though from long silence. I cried to his human shape

In that great wasteland: 'Living man or shade,
   Have pity and help me, whichever you may be!'
   'No living man, though once I was,' he replied.

'My parents both were Mantuans from Lombardy,
   And I was born *sub Julio*, the latter end.
   I lived in good Augustus's Rome, in the day

Of the false gods who lied. A poet, I hymned
   Anchises' noble son, who came from Troy
   When superb Ilium in its pride was burned.

But you – why go back down to such misery?
   Why not ascend the delightful mountain, source
   And principle that causes every joy?'

'Then are you Virgil? Are you the font that pours
   So overwhelming a river of human speech?'
   I answered, shamefaced. 'The glory and light are yours,

That poets follow – may the love that made me search
    Your book in patient study avail me, Master!
    You are my guide and author, whose verses teach

The graceful style whose model has done me honor.
    See this beast driving me backward – help me resist,
    For she makes all my veins and pulses shudder.'

'A different path from this one would be best
    For ou to find your way from this feral place,'
    He answered, seeing how I wept. 'This beast,

The cause of your complaint, lets no one pass
    Her way – but harries all to death. Her nature
    Is so malign and vicious she cannot appease

Her voracity, for feeding makes her hungrier.
    Many are the beasts she mates: there will be more,
    Until the Hound comes who will give this creature

A painful death. Not nourished by earthly fare,
    He will be fed by wisdom, goodness and love.
    Born between Feltro and Feltro, he shall restore

Low Italy, as Nisus fought to achieve.
    And Turnus, Euryalus, Camilla the maiden –
    All dead from wounds in war. He will remove

This lean wolf, hunting her through every region
    Till he has thrust her back to Hell's abyss
    Where Envy first dispatched her on her mission.

Therefore I judge it best that you should choose
    To follow me, and I will be your guide
    Away from here and through an eternal place:

To hear the cries of despair, and to behold
    Ancient tormented spirits as they lament
    In chorus the second death they must abide.

Then you shall see those souls who are content
    To dwell in fire because they hope some day
    To join the blessed: toward whom, if your ascent

Continues, your guide will be one worthier than I –
  When I must leave you, you will be with her.
  For the Emperor who governs from on high

Wills I not enter His city, where none may appear
  Who lived like me in rebellion to His law.
  His empire is everything and everywhere,

But that is His Kingdom, His city, His seat of awe.
  Happy is the soul He chooses for that place!'
  I: 'Poet, please – by the God you did not know –

Help me escape this evil that I face,
  And worse. Lead me to witness what you have said,
  Saint Peter's gate, and the multitude of woes – '

Then he set out, and I followed where he led.

DANTE ALIGHIERI
Translated from the Italian by Robert Pinsky

Inscription on the Monument of a Newfoundland Dog

Near this spot
Are deposited the Remains of one
Who possessed Beauty without Vanity,
Strength without Insolence,
Courage without Ferocity,
And all the Virtues of Man without his Vices.
This Praise, which would be unmeaning Flattery
If inscribed over human ashes,
Is but a just tribute to the Memory of
BOATSWAIN, a Dog,
Who was born at Newfoundland, May, 1803,
And died at Newstead Abbey, Nov. 18, 1808.

When some proud son of man returns to earth,
Unknown to glory, but upheld by birth,
The sculptor's art exhausts the pomp of woe,
And storied urns record who rests below;
When all is done, upon the tomb is seen,
Not what he was, but what he should have been:

But the poor dog, in life the firmest friend,
The first to welcome, foremost to defend,
Whose honest heart is still his master's own,
Who labours, fights, lives, breathes for him alone,
Unhonoured falls, unnoticed all his worth,
Denied in heaven the soul he held on earth:
While man, vain insect! hopes to be forgiven,
And claims himself a sole exclusive heaven.
Oh man! thou feeble tenant of an hour,
Debased by slavery, or corrupt by power,
Who knows thee well must quit thee with disgust,
Degraded mass of animated dust!
Thy love is lust, thy friendship all a cheat,
Thy smiles hypocrisy, thy words deceit!
By nature vile, ennobled but by name,
Each kindred brute might bid thee blush for shame.
Ye who perchance behold this simple urn,
Pass on – it honours none you wish to mourn:
To mark a friend's remains these stones arise,
I never knew but one, and here he lies.

LORD BYRON

Jabberwocky

'Twas brillig, and the slithy toves
    Did gyre and gimble in the wabe:
All mimsy were the borogoves,
    And the mome raths outgrabe.

'Beware the Jabberwock, my son!
    The jaws that bite, the claws that catch!
Beware the Jubjub bird, and shun
    The frumious Bandersnatch!'

He took his vorpal sword in hand:
    Long time the manxome foe he sought –
So rested he by the Tumtum tree,
    And stood awhile in thought.

And, as in uffish thought he stood,
    The Jabberwock, with eyes of flame,
Came whiffling through the tulgey wood,
    And burbled as it came!

One, two! One, two! And through and through
    The vorpal blade went snicker-snack!
He left it dead, and with its head
    He went galumphing back.

'And hast thou slain the Jabberwock?
    Come to my arms, my beamish boy!
O frabjous day! Callooh! Callay!'
    He chortled in his joy.

'Twas brillig, and the slithy toves
    Did gyre and gimble in the wabe:
All mimsy were the borogoves,
    And the mome raths outgrabe.

LEWIS CARROLL

A Jelly-Fish

Visible, invisible,
    a fluctuating charm
an amber-tinctured amethyst
    inhabits it, your arm
approaches and it opens
    and it closes; you had meant
to catch it and it quivers;
    you abandon your intent.

MARIANNE MOORE

Jim, Who Ran Away from His Nurse, and Was Eaten by a Lion

There was a boy whose name was Jim;
His friends were very good to him.
They gave him tea, and cakes, and jam,
And slices of delicious ham,
And chocolate with pink inside,
And little tricycles to ride,
And read him stories through and through,
And even took him to the Zoo –
But there it was the deadful fate
Befell him, which I now relate.

You know – at least you *ought* to know,
For I have often told you so –
That children never are allowed
To leave their nurses in a crowd;
Now this was Jim's especial foible,
He ran away when he was able,
And on this inauspicious day
He slipped his hand and ran away!
He hadn't gone a yard when – Bang!
With open jaws, a lion sprang,
And hungrily began to eat
The boy: beginning at his feet.

Now, just imagine how it feels
When first your toes and then your heels,
And then by gradual degrees,
Your shins and ankles, calves and knees,
Are slowly eaten, bit by bit.
No wonder Jim detested it!
No wonder that he shouted 'Hi!'
The honest keeper heard his cry,
Though very fat he almost ran
To help the little gentleman.
'Ponto!' he ordered as he came
(For Ponto was the lion's name),
'Ponto!' he cried, with angry frown.
'Let go, Sir! Down, Sir! Put it down!'

The lion made a sudden stop,
He let the dainty morsel drop,
And slunk reluctant to his cage,
Snarling with disappointed rage.
But when he bent him over Jim,
The honest keeper's eyes were dim.
The lion having reached his head,
The miserable boy was dead!

HILAIRE BELLOC

Kerr's Ass

We borrowed the loan of Kerr's big ass
To go to Dundalk with butter,
Brought him home the evening before the market
An exile that night in Mucker.

We heeled up the cart before the door,
We took the harness inside –
The straw-stuffed straddle, the broken breeching
With bits of bull-wire tied;

The winkers that had no choke-band,
The collar and the reins . . .
In Ealing Broadway, London Town
I name their several names

Until a world comes to life –
Morning, the silent bog,
And the God of imagination waking
In a Mucker fog.

PATRICK KAVANAGH

The Kilkenny Cats

There were once two cats of Kilkenny,
Each thought there was one cat too many;
So they fought and they fit,
And they scratched and they bit,
   Till, excepting their nails,
   And the tips of their tails,
Instead of two cats, there weren't any.

ANONYMOUS

The Kraken

Below the thunders of the upper deep,
Far, far beneath in the abysmal sea,
His ancient, dreamless, uninvaded sleep
The Kraken sleepeth: faintest sunlights flee
About his shadowy sides; above him swell
Huge sponges of millennial growth and height;
And far away into the sickly light,
From many a wondrous grot and secret cell
Unnumber'd and enormous polypi
Winnow with giant arms the slumbering green.
There hath he lain for ages, and will lie
Battening upon huge sea-worms in his sleep,
Until the latter fire shall heat the deep;
Then once by man and angels to be seen,
In roaring he shall rise and on the surface die.

ALFRED LORD TENNYSON

A Lady with a Falcon on her Fist

To the Honourable my Cousin, A. L.

This Queen of Prey (now Prey to you)
   Fast to that Pirch of Ivory
In silver Chaines and silken Clue
   Hath now made full thy Victory:

The swelling Admirall of the dread
   Cold Deepe, burnt in thy Flames, Oh Faire!
Wast not enough, but thou must lead
   Bound too the Princesse of the Aire?

Unarm'd of Wings and Scaly Oare,
   Unhappy Crawler on the Land,
To what Heav'n fly'st? div'st to what Shoare
   That her brave Eyes do not Command?

Ascend the Chariot of the Sun
   From her bright pow'r to shelter thee:
Her Captive (Foole) outgases him;
   Ah what lost wretches then are we!

Now, proud Usurpers on the Right
   Of sacred Beauty heare your dombe;
Recant your SEX, your MASTRY, MIGHT;
   Lower you cannot be or'ecome:

Repent, ye er'e nam'd HE or HEAD,
   For y' are in Falcons Monarchy,
And in that just Dominion bred,
   In which the NOBLER is the SHEE.

    RICHARD LOVELACE

The Lamb

   Little Lamb who made thee
   Dost thou know who made thee
Gave thee life & bid thee feed.

By the stream & o'er the mead;
Gave thee clothing of delight,
Softest clothing wooly bright;
Gave thee such a tender voice,
Making all the vales rejoice!
　　Little Lamb who made thee
　　Dost thou know who made thee
　　Little Lamb I'll tell thee,
　　Little Lamb I'll tell thee!
He is called by thy name,
For he calls himself a Lamb:
He is meek & he is mild,
He became a little child:
I a child & thou a lamb,
We are called by his name.
　　Little Lamb God bless thee.
　　Little Lamb God bless thee.

WILLIAM BLAKE

The Landrail

How sweet and pleasant grows the way
Through summer time again
While Landrails call from day to day
Amid the grass and grain

We hear it in the weeding time
When knee deep waves the corn
We hear it in the summers prime
Through meadows night and morn

And now I hear it in the grass
That grows as sweet again
And let a minutes notice pass
And now tis in the grain

Tis like a fancy every where
A sort of living doubt

We know tis somthing but it neer
Will blab the secret out

If heard in close or meadow plots
It flies if we pursue
But follows if we notice not
The close and meadow through

Boys know the note of many a bird
In their birdnesting bounds
But when the landrails noise is heard
They wonder at the sounds

They look in every tuft of grass
Thats in their rambles met
They peep in every bush they pass
And none the wiser get

And still they hear the craiking sound
And still they wonder why
It surely cant be under ground
Nor is it in the sky

And yet tis heard in every vale
An undiscovered song
And makes a pleasant wonder tale
For all the summer long

The shepherd whistles through his hands
And starts with many a whoop
His busy dog accross the lands
In hopes to fright it up

Tis still a minutes length or more
Till dogs are off and gone
Then sings and louder than before
But keeps the secret on

Yet accident will often meet
The nest within its way
And weeders when they weed the wheat
Discover where they lay

And mowers on the meadow lea

Chance on their noisey guest
And wonder what the bird can be
That lays without a nest

In simple holes that birds will rake
When dusting on the ground
They drop their eggs of curious make
Deep blotched and nearly round

A mystery still to men and boys
Who know not where they lay
And guess it but a summer noise
Among the meadow hay

JOHN CLARE

Leda and the Swan

A sudden blow: the great wings beating still
Above the staggering girl, her thighs caressed
By the dark webs, her nape caught in his bill,
He holds her helpless breast upon his breast.

How can those terrified vague fingers push
The feathered glory from her loosening thighs?
And how can body, laid in that white rush,
But feel the strange heart beating where it lies?

A shudder in the loins engenders there
The broken wall, the burning roof and tower
And Agamemnon dead.
                              Being so caught up,
So mastered by the brute blood of the air,
Did she put on his knowledge with his power
Before the indifferent beak could let her drop?

W. B. YEATS

Lines to a Dragon-Fly

Life (priest and poet say) is but a dream;
  I wish no happier one than to be laid
  Beneath a cool syringa's scented shade,
Or wavy willow, by the running stream,
  Brimful of moral, where the dragon-fly
  Wanders as careless and content as I.
Thanks for this fancy, insect king,
Of purple crest and filmy wing,
Who with indifference givest up
The water-lily's golden cup,
To come again and overlook
What I am writing in my book.
Believe me, most who read the line
Will read with hornier eyes than thine;
And yet their souls shall live for ever,
And thine drop dead into the river!
God pardon them, O insect king,
Who fancy so unjust a thing!

WALTER SAVAGE LANDOR

Little Miss Muffet

  Little Miss Muffet
  Sat on a tuffet,
Eating her curds and whey;
  There came a big spider,
  Who sat down beside her
And frightened Miss Muffet away.

ANONYMOUS

Little Trotty Wagtail

Little trotty wagtail he went in the rain
And tittering tottering sideways he near got straight again
He stooped to get a worm and look'd up to catch a fly
And then he flew away e're his feathers they were dry

Little trotty wagtail he waddled in the mud
And left his little foot marks trample where he would
He waddled in the water pudge and waggle went his tail
And chirrup up his wings to dry upon the garden rail

Little trotty wagtail you nimble all about
And in the dimpling water pudge you waddle in and out
Your home is nigh at hand and in the warm pigsty
So little Master Wagtail I'll bid you a 'Good bye'

JOHN CLARE

Littleblood

O littleblood, hiding from the mountains in the mountains
Wounded by stars and leaking shadow
Eating the medical earth.

O littleblood, little boneless little skinless
Ploughing with a linnet's carcase
Reaping the wind and threshing the stones.

O littleblood, drumming in a cow's skull
Dancing with a gnat's feet
With an elephant's nose with a crocodile's tail.

Grown so wise grown so terrible
Sucking death's mouldy tits.

Sit on my finger, sing in my ear, O littleblood.

TED HUGHES

Long-Legged Fly

That civilisation may not sink,
Its great battle lost,
Quiet the dog, tether the pony
To a distant post;
Our master Caesar is in the tent
Where the maps are spread,
His eyes fixed upon nothing,
A hand under his head.
Like a long-legged fly upon the stream
His mind moves upon silence.

That the topless towers be burnt
And men recall that face,
Move most gently if move you must
In this lonely place.
She thinks, part woman, three parts a child,
That nobody looks; her feet
Practise a tinker shuffle
Picked up on a street.
Like a long-legged fly upon the stream
Her mind moves upon silence.

That girls at puberty may find
The first Adam in their thought,
Shut the door of the Pope's chapel,
Keep those children out.
There on that scaffolding reclines
Michael Angelo.
With no more sound than the mice make
His hand moves to and fro.
Like a long-legged fly upon the stream
His mind moves upon silence.

W. B. YEATS

Lullaby for Titania

You spotted snakes with double tongue,
   Thorny hedgehogs, be not seen;
Newts, and blind-worms, do no wrong;
   Come not near our fairy queen.

    Philomel with melody
    Sing in our sweet lullaby;
Lulla, lulla, lullaby; lulla, lulla, lullaby!
Never harm, nor spell, nor charm,
    Come our lovely lady nigh!
    So good-night, with lullaby.

Weaving spiders, come not here;
   Hence, you long-legg'd spinners, hence:
Beetles black, approach not near;
   Worm, nor snail, do no offence.

    Philomel with melody
    Sing in our sweet lullaby;
Lulla, lulla, lullaby; lulla, lulla, lullaby!
Never harm, nor spell, nor charm,
    Come our lovely lady nigh!
    So good-night, with lullaby.

WILLIAM SHAKESPEARE

Lying in a Hammock at William Duffy's Farm in Pine Island, Minnesota

Over my head, I see the bronze butterfly,
Asleep on the black trunk,
Blowing like a leaf in green shadow.
Down the ravine behind the empty house,
The cowbells follow one another
Into the distances of the afternoon.
To my right,
In a field of sunlight between two pines,

The droppings of last year's horses
Blaze up into golden stones.
I lean back, as the evening darkens and comes on.
A chicken hawk floats over, looking for home.
I have wasted my life.

JAMES WRIGHT

The Maldive Shark

About the Shark, phlegmatical one,
Pale sot of the Maldive sea,
The sleek little pilot-fish, azure and slim,
How alert in attendance be.
From his saw-pit of mouth, from his charnel of maw,
They have nothing of harm to dread,
But liquidly glide on his ghastly flank
Or before his Gorgonian head;
Or lurk in the port of serrated teeth
In white triple tiers of glittering gates,
And there find a haven when peril's abroad,
An asylum in jaws of the Fates!
They are friends; and friendly they guide him to prey,
Yet never partake of the treat –
Eyes and brains to the dotard lethargic and dull,
Pale ravener of horrible meat.

HERMAN MELVILLE

The Man-Moth*

        Here, above,
cracks in the buildings are filled with battered moonlight.
The whole shadow of Man is only as big as his hat.
It lies at his feet like a circle for a doll to stand on,
and he makes an inverted pin, the point magnetized to the moon.

He does not see the moon; he observes only her vast properties,
feeling the queer light on his hands, neither warm nor cold,
of a temperature impossible to record in thermometers.

But when the Man-Moth
pays his rare, although occasional, visits to the surface,
the moon looks rather different to him. He emerges
from an opening under the edge of one of the sidewalks
and nervously begins to scale the faces of the buildings.
He thinks the moon is a small hole at the top of the sky,
proving the sky quite useless for protection.
He trembles, but must investigate as high as he can climb.

Up the façades,
his shadow dragging like a photographer's cloth behind him,
he climbs fearfully, thinking that this time he will manage
to push his small head through that round clean opening
and be forced through, as from a tube, in black scrolls on the light.
(Man, standing below him, has no such illusions.)
But what the Man-Moth fears most he must do, although
he fails, of course, and falls back scared but quite unhurt.

Then he returns
to the pale subways of cement he calls his home. He flits,
he flutters, and cannot get aboard the silent trains
fast enough to suit him. The doors close swiftly.
The Man-Moth always seats himself facing the wrong way
and the train starts at once at its full, terrible speed,
without a shift in gears or a gradation of any sort.
He cannot tell the rate at which he travels backwards.

Each night he must
be carried through artificial tunnels and dream recurrent dreams.
Just as the ties recur beneath his train, these underlie
his rushing brain. He does not dare look out the window,
for the third rail, the unbroken draught of poison,
runs there beside him. He regards it as a disease
he has inherited the susceptibility to. He has to keep
his hands in his pockets, as others must wear mufflers.

If you catch him,
hold up a flashlight to his eye. It's all dark pupil,

an entire night itself, whose haired horizon tightens
as he stares back, and closes up the eye. Then from the lids
one tear, his only possession, like the bee's sting, slips.
Slyly he palms it, and if you're not paying attention
he'll swallow it. However, if you watch, he'll hand it over,
cool as from underground springs and pure enough to drink.

ELIZABETH BISHOP
* Newspaper misprint for 'mammoth'.

Moly

Nightmare of beasthood, snorting, how to wake.
I woke. What beasthood skin she made me take?

Leathery toad that ruts for days on end,
Or cringing dribbling dog, man's servile friend,

Or cat that prettily pounces on its meat,
Tortures it hours, then does not care to eat:

Parrot, moth, shark, wolf, crocodile, ass, flea.
What germs, what jostling mobs there were in me.

These seem like bristles, and the hide is tough.
No claw or web here: each foot ends in hoof.

Into what bulk has method disappeared?
Like ham, streaked. I am gross – grey, gross, flap-eared.

The pale-lashed eyes my only human feature.
My teeth tear, tear. I am the snouted creature

That bites through anything, root, wire, or can.
If I was not afraid I'd eat a man.

Oh a man's flesh already is in mine.
Hand and foot poised for risk. Buried in swine.

I root and root, you think that it is greed,
It is, but I seek out a plant I need.

Direct me gods, whose changes are all holy,

To where it flickers deep in grass, the moly:

Cool flesh of magic in each leaf and shoot,
From milky flower to the black forked root.

From this fat dungeon I could rise to skin
And human title, putting pig within.

I push my big grey wet snout through the green,
Dreaming the flower I have never seen.

THOM GUNN

The Moose

For Grace Bulmer Bowers

From narrow provinces
of fish and bread and tea,
home of the long tides
where the bay leaves the sea
twice a day and takes
the herrings long rides,

where if the river
enters or retreats
in a wall of brown foam
depends on if it meets
the bay coming in,
the bay not at home;

where, silted red,
sometimes the sun sets
facing a red sea,
and others, veins the flats'
lavender, rich mud
in burning rivulets;

on red, gravelly roads,
down rows of sugar maples,
past clapboard farmhouses

and neat, clapboard churches,
bleached, ridged as clamshells,
past twin silver birches,

through late afternoon
a bus journeys west,
the windshield flashing pink,
pink glancing off of metal,
brushing the dented flank
of blue, beat-up enamel;

down hollows, up rises,
and waits, patient, while
a lone traveller gives
kisses and embraces
to seven relatives
and a collie supervises.

Goodbye to the elms,
to the farm, to the dog.
The bus starts. The light
grows richer; the fog,
shifting, salty, thin,
comes closing in.

Its cold, round crystals
form and slide and settle
in the white hens' feathers,
in gray glazed cabbages,
on the cabbage roses
and lupins like apostles;

the sweet peas cling
to their wet white string
on the whitewashed fences;
bumblebees creep
inside the foxgloves,
and evening commences.

One stop at Bass River.
Then the Economies –
Lower, Middle, Upper;

Five Islands, Five Houses,
where a woman shakes a tablecloth
out after supper.

A pale flickering. Gone.
The Tantramar marshes
and the smell of salt hay.
An iron bridge trembles
and a loose plank rattles
but doesn't give way.

On the left, a red light
swims through the dark:
a ship's port lantern.
Two rubber boots show,
illuminated, solemn.
A dog gives one bark.

A woman climbs in
with two market bags,
brisk, freckled, elderly.
'A grand night. Yes, sir,
all the way to Boston.'
She regards us amicably.

Moonlight as we enter
the New Brunswick woods,
hairy, scratchy, splintery;
moonlight and mist
caught in them like lamb's wool
on bushes in a pasture.

The passengers lie back.
Snores. Some long sighs.
A dreamy divagation
begins in the night,
a gentle, auditory,
slow hallucination . . .

In the creakings and noises,
an old conversation
– not concerning us,

but recognizable, somewhere,
back in the bus:
Grandparents' voices

uninterruptedly
talking, in Eternity:
names being mentioned,
things cleared up finally;
what he said, what she said,
who got pensioned;

deaths, deaths and sicknesses;
the year he remarried;
the year (something) happened.
She died in childbirth.
That was the son lost
when the schooner foundered.

He took to drink. Yes.
She went to the bad.
When Amos began to pray
even in the store and
finally the family had
to put him away.

'Yes . . .' that peculiar
affirmative. 'Yes . . .'
A sharp, indrawn breath,
half groan, half acceptance,
that means 'Life's like that.
We know *it* (also death).'

Talking the way they talked
in the old featherbed,
peacefully, on and on,
dim lamplight in the hall,
down in the kitchen, the dog
tucked in her shawl.

Now, it's all right now
even to fall asleep
just as on all those nights.

– Suddenly the bus driver
stops with a jolt,
turns off his lights.

A moose has come out of
the impenetrable wood
and stands there, looms, rather,
in the middle of the road.
It approaches; it sniffs at
the bus's hot hood.

Towering, antlerless,
high as a church,
homely as a house
(or, safe as houses).
A man's voice assures us
'Perfectly harmless . . .'

Some of the passengers
exclaim in whispers,
childishly, softly,
'Sure are big creatures.'
'It's awful plain.'
'Look! It's a she!'

Taking her time,
she looks the bus over,
grand, otherworldly.
Why, why do we feel
(we all feel) this sweet
sensation of joy?

'Curious creatures,'
says our quiet driver,
rolling his *r*'s.
'Look at that, would you.'
Then he shifts gears.
For a moment longer,

by craning backward,
the moose can be seen
on the moonlit macadam;

then there's a dim
smell of moose, an acrid
smell of gasoline.

ELIZABETH BISHOP

The Most of It

He thought he kept the universe alone;
For all the voice in answer he could wake
Was but the mocking echo of his own
From some tree-hidden cliff across the lake.
Some morning from the boulder-broken beach
He would cry out on life, that what it wants
Is not its own love back in copy speech,
But counter-love, original response.
And nothing ever came of what he cried
Unless it was the embodiment that crashed
In the cliff's talus on the other side,
And then in the far-distant water splashed,
But after a time allowed for it to swim,
Instead of proving human when it neared
And someone else additional to him,
As a great buck it powerfully appeared,
Pushing the crumpled water up ahead,
And landed pouring like a waterfall,
And stumbled through the rocks with horny tread,
And forced the underbrush – and that was all.

ROBERT FROST

Mountain Lion

Climbing through the January snow, into the Lobo canyon
Dark grow the spruce-trees, blue is the balsam, water sounds still
    unfrozen, and the trail is still evident.

Men!
Two men!
Men! The only animal in the world to fear!

They hesitate.
We hesitate.
They have a gun.
We have no gun.

Then we all advance, to meet.

Two Mexicans, strangers, emerging out of the dark and snow and
    inwardness of the Lobo valley.
What are they doing here on this vanishing trail?

What is he carrying?
Something yellow.
A deer?

Qué tiene, amigo?
León –

He smiles, foolishly, as if he were caught doing wrong.
And we smile, foolishly, as if we didn't know.
He is quite gentle and dark-faced.

It is a mountain lion,
A long, long slim cat, yellow like a lioness.
Dead.

He trapped her this morning, he says, smiling foolishly.
Lift up her face,
Her round, bright face, bright as frost.
Her round, fine-fashioned head, with two dead ears;
And stripes in the brilliant frost of her face, sharp, fine dark rays,
Dark, keen, fine rays in the brilliant frost of her face.
Beautiful dead eyes.

Hermoso es!

They go out towards the open;
We go on into the gloom of Lobo.
And above the trees I found her lair,
A hole in the blood-orange brilliant rocks that stick up, a little cave.
And bones, and twigs, and a perilous ascent.

So, she will never leap up that way again, with the yellow flash of a
    mountain lion's long shoot!
And her bright striped frost-face will never watch any more, out of the
    shadow of the cave in the blood-orange rock,
Above the trees of the Lobo dark valley-mouth!

Instead, I look out.
And out to the dim of the desert, like a dream, never real;
To the snow of the Sangre de Cristo mountains, the ice of the mountains
    of Picoris,
And near across at the opposite steep of snow, green trees motionless
    standing in snow, like a Christmas toy.

And I think in this empty world there was room for me and a mountain
    lion.
And I think in the world beyond, how easily we might spare a million
    or two of humans
And never miss them.
Yet what a gap in the world, the missing white frost-face of that slim
    yellow mountain lion!

D. H. LAWRENCE

The Mouse's Nest

I found a ball of grass among the hay
And proged it as I passed and went away
And when I looked I fancied somthing stirred
And turned agen and hoped to catch the bird
When out an old mouse bolted in the wheat
With all her young ones hanging at her teats
She looked so odd and so grotesque to me
I ran and wondered what the thing could be
And pushed the knapweed bunches where I stood
When the mouse hurried from the crawling brood
The young ones squeaked and when I went away
She found her nest again among the hay
The water oer the pebbles scarce could run
And broad old cesspools glittered in the sun

JOHN CLARE

The Mower

The mower stalled, twice; kneeling, I found
A hedgehog jammed up against the blades,
Killed. It had been in the long grass.

I had seen it before, and even fed it, once.
Now I had mauled its unobtrusive world
Unmendably. Burial was no help:

Next morning I got up and it did not.
The first day after a death, the new absence
Is always the same; we should be careful

Of each other, we should be kind
While there is still time.

PHILIP LARKIN

The Mower to the Glowworms

Ye living lamps, by whose dear light
The nightingale does sit so late,
And studying all the summer night,
Her matchless songs does meditate;

Ye country comets, that portend
No war, nor prince's funeral,
Shining unto no higher end
Than to presage the grass's fall;

Ye glowworms, whose officious flame
To wandering mowers shows the way,
That in the night have lost their aim,
And after foolish fires do stray;

Your courteous lights in vain you waste,
Since Juliana here is come,
For she my mind hath so displaced
That I shall never find my home.

ANDREW MARVELL

Mr Edwards and the Spider

I saw the spiders marching through the air,
Swimming from tree to tree that mildewed day
    In latter August when the hay
    Came creaking to the barn. But where
        The wind is westerly,
Where gnarled November makes the spiders fly
Into the apparitions of the sky,
They purpose nothing but their ease and die
Urgently beating east to sunrise and the sea;

What are we in the hands of the great God?
It was in vain you set up thorn and briar
    In battle array against the fire
    And treason crackling in your blood;
        For the wild thorns grow tame
And will do nothing to oppose the flame;
Your lacerations tell the losing game
You play against a sickness past your cure.
How will the hands be strong? How will the heart endure?

A very little thing, a little worm,
Or hourglass-blazoned spider, it is said,
    Can kill a tiger. Will the dead
    Hold up his mirror and affirm
        To the four winds the smell
And flash of his authority? It's well
If God who holds you to the pit of hell,
Much as one holds a spider, will destroy,
Baffle and dissipate your soul. As a small boy

On Windsor Marsh, I saw the spider die
When thrown into the bowels of fierce fire:
    There's no long struggle, no desire
    To get up on its feet and fly –
        It stretches out its feet

And dies. This is the sinner's last retreat;
Yes, and no strength exerted on the heat
  Then sinews the abolished will, when sick
And full of burning, it will whistle on a brick.

  But who can plumb the sinking of that soul?
  Josiah Hawley, picture yourself cast
    Into a brick-kiln where the blast
    Fans your quick vitals to a coal –
      If measured by a glass,
  How long would it seem burning! Let there pass
  A minute, ten, ten trillion; but the blaze
  Is infinite, eternal: this is death,
To die and know it. This is the Black Widow, death.

ROBERT LOWELL

My Cat Jeoffry

For I will consider my cat Jeoffry.

For he is the servant of the Living God duly and daily serving him.

For at the first glance of the glory of God in the East he worships in
    his way.

For is this done by wreathing his body seven times round with elegant
    quickness.

For then he leaps up to catch the musk, which is the blessing of God
    upon his prayer.

For he rolls upon prank to work it in.

For having done duty and received blessing he begins to consider
    himself.

For this he performs in ten degrees.

For first he looks upon his fore-paws to see if they are clean.

For secondly he kicks up behind to clear away there.

For thirdly he works it upon stretch with the fore paws extended.

For fourthly he sharpens his paws by wood.

For fifthly he washes himself.

For sixthly he rolls upon wash.

For seventhly he fleas himself, that he may not be interrupted upon
    the beat.

For eighthly he rubs himself against a post.

For ninthly he looks up for his instructions.

For tenthly he goes in quest of food.

For having consider'd God and himself he will consider his neighbour.

For if he meets another cat he will kiss her in kindness.

For when he takes his prey he plays with it to give it a chance.

For one mouse in seven escapes by his dallying.

For when his day's work is done his business more properly begins.

For he keeps the Lord's watch in the night against the adversary.

For he counteracts the powers of darkness by his electrical skin and glaring eyes.

For he counteracts the Devil, who is death, by brisking about the life.

For in his morning orisons he loves the sun and the sun loves him.

For he is of the tribe of Tiger.

For the Cherub Cat is a term of the Angel Tiger.

For he has the subtlety and hissing of a serpent, which in goodness he suppresses.

For he will not do destruction, if he is well-fed, neither will he spit without provocation.

For he purrs in thankfulness, when God tells him he's a good cat.

For he is an instrument for the children to learn benevolence upon.

For every house is incomplete without him and a blessing is lacking in the spirit.

For the Lord commanded Moses concerning the cats at the departure of the Children of Israel from Egypt.

For every family had one cat at least in the bag.

For the English cats are the best in Europe.

For he is the cleanest in the use of his fore-paws of any quadrupede.

For the dexterity of his defence is an instance of the love of God to him exceedingly.

For he is the quickest to his mark of any creature.

For he is tenacious of his point.

For he is a mixture of gravity and waggery.

For he knows that God is his Saviour.

For there is nothing sweeter than his peace when at rest.

For there is nothing brisker than his life when in motion.

For he is of the Lord's poor and so indeed is he called by benevolence
perpetually – Poor Jeoffry! poor Jeoffry! the rat has bit thy throat.

For I bless the name of the Lord Jesus that Jeoffry is better.

For the divine spirit comes about his body to sustain it in complete
cat.

For his tongue is exceeding pure so that it has in purity what it wants
in music.

For he is docile and can learn certain things.

For he can set up with gravity which is patience upon approbation.

For he can fetch and carry, which is patience in employment.

For he can jump over a stick which is patience upon proof positive.

For he can spraggle upon waggle at the word of command.

For he can jump from an eminence into his master's bosom.

For he can catch the cork and toss it again.

For he is hated by the hypocrite and miser.

For the former is afraid of detection.

For the latter refuses the charge.

For he camels his back to bear the first notion of business.

For he is good to think on, if a man would express himself neatly.

For he made a great figure in Egypt for his signal services.

For he killed the Ichneumon-rat very pernicious by land.

For his ears are so acute that they sting again.

For from this proceeds the passing quickness of his attention.

For by stroaking of him I have found out electricity.

For I perceived God's light about him both wax and fire.

For the Electrical fire is the spiritual substance, which God sends from
heaven to sustain the bodies both of man and beast.

For God has blessed him in the variety of his movements.

For, tho he cannot fly, he is an excellent clamberer.

For his motions upon the face of the earth are more than any other
quadrupede.

For he can tread to all the measures upon the music.

For he can swim for life.

For he can creep.

CHRISTOPHER SMART

A Name for All

Moonmoth and grasshopper that flee our page
And still wing on, untarnished of the name
We pinion to your bodies to assuage
Our envy of your freedom – we must maim

Because we are usurpers, and chagrined –
And take the wing and scar it in the hand.
Names we have, even, to clap on the wind;
But we must die, as you, to understand.

I dreamed that all men dropped their names, and sang
As only they can praise, who build their days
With fin and hoof, with wing and sweetened fang
Struck free and holy in one Name always.

HART CRANE

The Names of the Hare

The man the hare has met
will never be the better of it
except he lay down on the land
what he carries in his hand –
be it staff or be it bow –
and bless him with his elbow
and come out with this litany
with devotion and sincerity
to speak the praises of the hare.
Then the man will better fare.

'The hare, call him scotart,
big-fellow, bouchart,
the O'Hare, the jumper,
the rascal, the racer.

Beat-the-pad, white-face,
funk-the-ditch, shit-ass.

The wimount, the messer,
the skidaddler, the nibbler,
the ill-met, the slabber.

The quick-scut, the dew-flirt,
the grass-biter, the goibert,
the home-late, the do-the-dirt.

The starer, the wood-cat,
the purblind, the furze cat,
the skulker, the bleary-eyed,
the wall-eyed, the glance-aside
and also the hedge-springer.

The stubble-stag, the long lugs,
the stook-deer, the frisky legs,
the wild one, the skipper,
the hug-the-ground, the lurker,
the race-the-wind, the skiver,
the shag-the-hare, the hedge-squatter,
the dew-hammer, the dew-hopper,
the sit-tight, the grass-bounder,
the jig-foot, the earth-sitter,
the light-foot, the fern-sitter,
the kail-stag, the herb-cropper.

The creep-along, the sitter-still,
the pintail, the ring-the-hill,
the sudden start,
the shake-the-heart,
the belly-white,
the lambs-in-flight.

The gobshite, the gum-sucker,
the scare-the-man, the faith-breaker,
the snuff-the-ground, the baldy skull,
(his chief name is scoundrel.)

The stag sprouting a suede horn,
the creature living in the corn,
the creature bearing all men's scorn,
the creature no one dares to name.'

When you have got all this said
then the hare's strength has been laid.
Then you might go faring forth –
east and west and south and north,
wherever you incline to go –
but only if you're skilful too.
And now, Sir Hare, good-day to you.
God guide you to a how-d'ye-do
with me: come to me dead
in either onion broth or bread.

ANONYMOUS
Translated from the Middle English by Seamus Heaney

'A narrow Fellow in the Grass'

A narrow Fellow in the Grass
Occasionally rides –
You may have met Him – did you not
His notice sudden is –

The Grass divides as with a Comb –
A spotted shaft is seen –
And then it closes at your feet
And opens further on –

He likes a Boggy Acre
A Floor too cool for Corn –
Yet when a Boy, and Barefoot –
I more than once at Noon
Have passed, I thought, a Whip lash
Unbraiding in the Sun
When stooping to secure it
It wrinkled, and was gone –

Several of Nature's people
I know, and they know me –
I feel for them a transport
Of cordiality –

But never met this Fellow
Attended, or alone
Without a tighter breathing
And Zero at the Bone –

EMILY DICKINSON

Never Again Would Birds' Song Be the Same

He would declare and could himself believe
That the birds there in all the garden round
From having heard the daylong voice of Eve
Had added to their own an oversound,
Her tone of meaning but without the words.
Admittedly an eloquence so soft
Could only have had an influence on birds
When call or laughter carried it aloft.
Be that as may be, she was in their song.
Moreover her voice upon their voices crossed
Had now persisted in the woods so long
That probably it never would be lost.
Never again would birds' song be the same.
And to do that to birds was why she came.

ROBERT FROST

The Nightingale

A Conversation Poem. April 1798

No cloud, no relique of the sunken day
Distinguishes the West, no long thin slip
Of sullen light, no obscure trembling hues.
Come, we will rest on this old mossy bridge!
You see the glimmer of the stream beneath,
But hear no murmuring: it flows silently,
O'er its soft bed of verdure. All is still,

A balmy night! and though the stars be dim,
Yet let us think upon the vernal showers
That gladden the green earth, and we shall find
A pleasure in the dimness of the stars.
And hark! the Nightingale begins its song,
'Most musical, most melancholy' bird!
A melancholy bird? Oh! idle thought!
In nature there is nothing melancholy.
But some night-wandering man, whose heart was pierced
With the remembrance of a grievous wrong,
Or slow distemper, or neglected love,
(And so, poor wretch! filled all things with himself,
And made all gentle sounds tell back the tale
Of his own sorrow) he, and such as he,
First named these notes a melancholy strain.
And many a poet echoes the conceit;
Poet who hath been building up the rhyme
When he had better far have stretched his limbs
Beside a brook in mossy forest-dell,
By sun or moon-light, to the influxes
Of shapes and sounds and shifting elements
Surrendering his whole spirit, of his song
And of his fame forgetful! so his fame
Should share in Nature's immortality,
A venerable thing! and so his song
Should make all Nature lovelier, and itself
Be loved like Nature! But 'twill not be so;
And youths and maidens most poetical,
Who lose the deepening twilights of the spring
In ball-rooms and hot theatres, they still
Full of meek sympathy must heave their sighs
O'er Philomela's pity-pleading strains.

My Friend, and thou, our Sister! we have learnt
A different lore: we may not thus profane
Nature's sweet voices, always full of love
And joyance! 'Tis the merry Nightingale
That crowds, and hurries, and precipitates
With fast thick warble his delicious notes,
As he were fearful that an April night

Would be too short for him to utter forth
His love-chant, and disburthen his full soul
Of all its music!

                    And I know a grove
Of large extent, hard by a castle huge,
Which the great lord inhabits not; and so
This grove is wild with tangling underwood,
And the trim walks are broken up, and grass,
Thin grass and king-cups grow within the paths.
But never elsewhere in one place I knew
So many nightingales; and far and near,
In wood and thicket, over the wide grove,
They answer and provoke each other's song,
With skirmish and capricious passagings,
And murmurs musical and swift jug jug,
And one low piping sound more sweet than all –
Stirring the air with such a harmony,
That should you close your eyes, you might almost
Forget it was not day! On moonlight bushes,
Whose dewy leaflets are but half-disclosed,
You may perchance behold them on the twigs,
Their bright, bright eyes, their eyes both bright and full,
Glistening, while many a glow-worm in the shade
Lights up her love-torch.

                    A most gentle Maid,
Who dwelleth in her hospitable home
Hard by the castle, and at latest eve
(Even like a Lady vowed and dedicate
To something more than Nature in the grove)
Glides through the pathways; she knows all their notes,
That gentle Maid! and oft a moment's space,
What time the moon was lost behind a cloud,
Hath heard a pause of silence; till the moon
Emerging, hath awakened earth and sky
With one sensation, and those wakeful birds
Have all burst forth in choral minstrelsy,
As if some sudden gale had swept at once
A hundred airy harps! And she hath watched
Many a nightingale perch giddily

On blossomy twig still swinging from the breeze,
And to that motion tune his wanton song
Like tipsy Joy that reels with tossing head.

Farewell, O Warbler! till to-morrow eve,
And you, my friends! farewell, a short farewell!
We have been loitering long and pleasantly,
And now for our dear homes. – That strain again!
Full fain it would delay me! My dear babe,
Who, capable of no articulate sound,
Mars all things with his imitative lisp,
How he would place his hand beside his ear,
His little hand, the small forefinger up,
And bid us listen! And I deem it wise
To make him Nature's play-mate. He knows well
The evening-star; and once, when he awoke
In most distressful mood (some inward pain
Had made up that strange thing, an infant's dream, –)
I hurried with him to our orchard-plot,
And he beheld the moon, and, hushed at once,
Suspends his sobs, and laughs most silently,
While his fair eyes, that swam with undropped tears,
Did glitter in the yellow moon-beam! Well! –
It is a father's tale: But if that Heaven
Should give me life, his childhood shall grow up
Familiar with these songs, that with the night
He may associate joy. – Once more, farewell,
Sweet Nightingale! once more, my friends! farewell.

SAMUEL TAYLOR COLERIDGE

The Nightingale

The nightingale, as soon as April bringeth
Unto her rested sense a perfect waking,
While late bare earth, proud of new clothing, springeth,
Sings out her woes, a thorn her song-book making,
And mournfully bewailing,

Her throat in tunes expresseth
For Tereus' force on her chaste will prevailing.
Oh Philomela fair, Oh take some gladness,
That here is juster cause of plaintful sadness:
Thine earth now springs, mine fadeth;
Thy thorn without, my thorn my heart invadeth.

Alas, she hath no other cause of anguish
But Tereus' love, on her by strong hand wroken,
Wherein she suffering, all her spirits languish;
Full womanlike complains her will was broken.
But I, who daily craving,
Cannot have to content me,
Have more cause to lament me,
Since wanting is more woe than too much having.
O Philomela fair, O take some gladness,
That here is juster cause of plaintful sadness:
Thine earth now springs, mine fadeth;
Thy thorn without, my thorn my heart invadeth.

PHILIP SIDNEY

A Noiseless Patient Spider

A noiseless patient spider,
I mark'd where on a little promontory it stood isolated,
It launch'd forth filament, filament, filament, out of itself,
Ever unreeling them, ever tirelessly speeding them.

And you O my soul where you stand,
Surrounded, detached, in measureless oceans of space,
Ceaselessly musing, venturing, throwing, seeking the spheres to connect
    them,
Till the bridge you will need be form'd, till the ductile anchor hold,
Till the gossamer thread you fling catch somewhere, O my soul.

WALT WHITMAN

The Nun's Lament for Philip Sparrow

When I remember'd again
How my Philip was slain,
I wept and I wailed,
The tears down hailed;
But nothing it avail'd
To call Philip again
Whom Gib our cat hath slain.
   Heu, heu, me,
That I am woe for thee!
Levavi oculos meos in montis,
Would that I had Xenophontis
Or Socrates the Wise,
To show me their device
Moderately to take
This sorrow that I make
For Philip Sparrow's sake!
   It had a velvet cap,
And would sit on my lap,
And seek after small worms,
And sometimes white bread crumbs;
And many times and oft
Within my breast soft
It would lie and rest.
   Sometimes he would gasp
When he saw a wasp;
A fly or a gnat,
He would fly at that;
And prettily he would pant
When he saw an ant;
Lord, how he would pry
After the butterfly!
Lord, how he would hop
After the grasshop!
And when I said, Phip, Phip,
Then he would leap and skip,
And take me by the lip.
   De profundis clamavi

When I saw my sparrow die.
   Vengeance I ask and cry,
By way of exclamation,
On all the whole nation
Of cats wild and tame;
That cat especially
That slew so cruelly
My little pretty sparrow
That I brought up at Carow.
   O cat of churlish kind,
The fiend was in thy mind.
I would thou hadst been blind!
The leopards savage,
The lions in their rage,
May they catch thee in their paws,
And gnaw thee in their jaws;
The dragons with their tongues
May they poison thy liver and lungs.
Of India the greedy gripes
May they tear out all thy tripes;
Of Arcady the bears
May they pluck away thine ears;
The wild wolf Lycaon
Bite asunder thy back-bone;
Of Ætna the burning hill,
That night and day burneth still,
Set thy tail in a blaze,
That all the world may gaze
And wonder upon thee,
From Ocean, the great sea,
Unto the Isles of Orchadye;
From Tilbury Ferry
To the plain of Salisbury.

   JOHN SKELTON

The Nymph Complaining for the Death of her Faun

The wanton Troopers riding by
Have shot my Faun and it will dye.
Ungentle men! They cannot thrive
To kill thee. Thou neer didst alive
Them any harm: alas nor cou'd
Thy death yet do them any good.
I'me sure I never wisht them ill;
Nor do I for all this; nor will:
But, if my simple Pray'rs may yet
Prevail with Heaven to forget
Thy murder, I will Joyn my Tears
Rather then fail. But, O my fears!
It cannot dye so. Heavens King
Keeps register of every thing:
And nothing may we use in vain.
Ev'n Beasts must be with justice slain;
Else Men are made their *Deodands*.
Though they should wash their guilty hands
In this warm life blood, which doth part
From thine, and wound me to the Heart,
Yet could they not be clean: their Stain
Is dy'd in such a Purple Grain.
There is not such another in
The World, to offer for their Sin.
    Unconstant *Sylvio*, when yet
I had not found him counterfeit,
One morning (I remember well)
Ty'd in this silver Chain and Bell,
Gave it to me: nay and I know
What he said then; I'me sure I do.
Said He, look how your Huntsman here
Hath taught a Faun to hunt his *Dear*.
But *Sylvio* soon had me beguil'd.
This waxed tame; while he grew wild,
And quite regardless of my Smart,
Left me his Faun, but took his Heart.
    Thenceforth I set my self to play

My solitary time away,
With this: and very well content,
Could so mine idle Life have spent
For it was full of sport; and light
Of foot, and heart; and did invite,
Me to its game; it seem'd to bless
Its self in me. How could I less
Than love it? O I cannot be
Unkind, t' a Beast that loveth me.

   Had it liv'd long, I do not know
Whether it too might have done so
As *Sylvio* did: his Gifts might be
Perhaps as false or more than he.
But I am sure, for ought that I
Could in so short a time espie,
Thy Love was far more better then
The love of false and cruel men.

   With sweetest milk, and sugar, first
I it at mine own fingers nurst.
And as it grew, so every day
It wax'd more white and sweet than they.
It had so sweet a Breath! And oft
I blusht to see its foot more soft,
And white, (shall I say then my hand?)
NAY any Ladies of the Land.

   It is a wond'rous thing, how fleet
'Twas on those little silver feet.
With what a pretty skipping grace,
It oft would challenge me the Race:
And when 'thad left me far away,
'Twould stay, and run again, and stay.
For it was nimbler much than Hindes;
And trod, as on the four Winds.

   I have a Garden of my own,
But so with Roses over grown,
And Lillies, that you would it guess
To be a little Wilderness.
And all the Spring time of the year
It onely loved to be there.
Among the beds of Lillyes, I

Have sought it oft, where it should lye;
Yet could not, till it self would rise,
Find it, although before mine Eyes.
For, in the flaxen Lillies shade,
It like a bank of Lillies laid.
Upon the Roses it would feed,
Until its Lips ev'n seem'd to bleed:
And then to me 'twould boldly trip,
And print those Roses on my Lip.
But all its chief delight was still
On Roses thus its self to fill:
And its pure virgin Limbs to fold
In whitest sheets of Lillies cold.
Had it liv'd long, it would have been
Lillies without, Roses within.

O help! O help! I see it faint:
And dye as calmely as a Saint.
See how it weeps. The Tears do come
Sad, slowly dropping like a Gumme.
So weeps the wounded Balsome: so
The holy Frankincense doth flow.
The brotherless *Heliades*
Melt in such Amber Tears as these.

I in a golden Vial will
Keep these two crystal Tears; and fill
It till it do o'reflow with mine;
Then place it in *Diana's* Shrine.

Now my sweet Faun is vanish'd to
Whether the Swans and Turtles go:
In fair *Elizium* to endure,
With milk-white Lambs, and Ermins pure.
O do not run too fast: for I
Will but bespeak they Grave, and dye.

First my unhappy Statue shall
Be cut in Marble; and withal,
Let it be weeping too: but there
Th' Engraver sure his Art may spare;
For I so truly thee bemoane,
That I shall weep though I be Stone:
Until my Tears, still dropping, wear

My breast, themselves engraving there.
There at my feet shalt thou be laid,
Of purest Alabaster made:
For I would have thine Image be
White as I can, though not as Thee.

ANDREW MARVELL

'O Nightingale'

O Nightingale, that on yon bloomy Spray
    Warbl'st at eeve, when all the Woods are still,
    Thou with fresh hope the Lovers heart dost fill,
    While the jolly hours lead on propitious *May*;
Thy liquid notes that close the eye of Day,
    First heard before the shallow Cuccoo's bill
    Portend success in love; O if *Jove*'s will
    Have linkt that amorous power to thy soft lay,
Now timely sing, ere the rude Bird of Hate
    Foretell my hopeles doom in som Grove nigh:
    As thou from yeer to yeer hast sung too late
For my relief; yet hadst no reason why.
    Whether the Muse, or Love call thee his mate,
    Both them I serve, and of their train am I.

JOHN MILTON

October Salmon

He's lying in poor water, a yard or so depth of poor safety,
Maybe only two feet under the no-protection of an outleaning small
    oak,
Half-under a tangle of brambles.

After his two thousand miles, he rests,
Breathing in that lap of easy current
In his graveyard pool.

About six pounds weight,
Four years old at most, and hardly a winter at sea –
But already a veteran,
Already a death-patched hero. So quickly it's over!

So briefly he roamed the gallery of marvels!
Such sweet months, so richly embroidered into earth's beauty-dress,
Her life-robe –
Now worn out with her tirelessness, her insatiable quest,
Hangs in the flow, a frayed scarf –

An autumnal pod of his flower,
The mere hull of his prime, shrunk at shoulder and flank,

With the sea-going Aurora Borealis of his April power –
The primrose and violet of that first upfling in the estuary –
Ripened to muddy dregs,
The river reclaiming his sea-metals.

In the October light
He hangs there, patched with leper-cloths.

Death has already dressed him
In her clownish regimentals, her badges and decorations,
Mapping the completion of his service,
His face a ghoul-mask, a dinosaur of senility, and his whole body
A fungoid anemone of canker –

Can the caress of water ease him?
The flow will not let up for a minute.

What a change! from that covenant of Polar Light
To this shroud in a gutter!
What a death-in-life – to be his own spectre!
His living body become death's puppet,
Dolled by death in her crude paints and drapes
He haunts his own staring vigil
And suffers the subjection, and the dumbness,
And the humiliation of the role!

And that is how it is,
That is what is going on there, under the scrubby oak tree, hour after
    hour,

That is what the splendour of the sea has come down to,
And the eye of ravenous joy – king of infinite liberty
In the flashing expanse, the bloom of sea-life,

On the surge-ride of energy, weightless,
Body simply the armature of energy
In that earliest sea-freedom, the savage amazement of life,
The salt mouthful of actual existence
With strength like light –

Yet this was always with him. This was inscribed in his egg.
This chamber of horrors is also home.
He was probably hatched in this very pool.

And this was the only mother he ever had, this uneasy channel of
    minnows
Under the mill-wall, with bicycle wheels, car-tyres, bottles
And sunk sheets of corrugated iron.
People walking their dogs trail their evening shadows across him.
If boys see him they will try to kill him.

All this, too, is stitched into the torn richness,
The epic poise
That holds him so steady in his wounds, so loyal to his doom, so
    patient
In the machinery of heaven.

    TED HUGHES

Ode on the Death of a Favourite Cat, Drowned in a Tub of Goldfishes

'Twas on a lofty vase's side,
Where China's gayest art had dyed
    The azure flowers that blow;
Demurest of the tabby kind,
The pensive Selima, reclined,
    Gazed on the lake below.

Her conscious tail her joy declared;
The fair round face, the snowy beard,
    The velvet of her paws,
Her coat, that with the tortoise vies,
Her ears of jet, and emerald eyes,
    She saw; and purred applause.

Still had she gazed; but 'midst the tide
Two angel forms were seen to glide,
    The genii of the stream:
Their scaly armour's Tyrian hue
Through richest purple to the view
    Betrayed a golden gleam.

The hapless nymph with wonder saw:
A whisker first and then a claw,
    With many an ardent wish,
She stretched in vain to reach the prize.
What female heart can gold despise?
    What cat's averse to fish?

Presumptuous maid! with looks intent
Again she stretched, again she bent,
    Nor knew the gulf between.
(Malignant Fate sat by and smiled)
The slippery verge her feet beguiled,
    She tumbled headlong in.

Eight times emerging from the flood
She mewed to every watery god,
    Some speedy aid to send.
No dolphin came, no Nereïd stirred;
Nor cruel Tom, nor Susan heard;
    A favourite has no friend!

From hence, ye beauties, undeceived,
Know, one false step is ne'er retrieved,
    And be with caution bold.
Not all that tempts your wandering eyes
And heedless hearts, is lawful prize;
    Nor all that glisters, gold.

THOMAS GRAY

Ode to a Nightingale

My heart aches, and a drowsy numbness pains
  My sense, as though of hemlock I had drunk,
Or emptied some dull opiate to the drains
  One minute past, and Lethe-wards had sunk:
'Tis not through envy of thy happy lot,
  But being too happy in thine happiness, –
    That thou, light-winged Dryad of the trees,
      In some melodious plot
  Of beechen green, and shadows numberless,
    Singest of summer in full-throated ease.

O, for a draught of vintage! that hath been
  Cool'd a long age in the deep-delved earth,
Tasting of Flora and the country green,
  Dance, and Provençal song, and sunburnt mirth!
O for a beaker full of the warm South,
  Full of the true, the blushful Hippocrene,
    With beaded bubbles winking at the brim,
      And purple-stained mouth;
  That I might drink, and leave the world unseen,
    And with thee fade away into the forest dim:

Fade far away, dissolve, and quite forget
  What thou among the leaves hast never known,
The weariness, the fever, and the fret
  Here, where men sit and hear each other groan;
Where palsy shakes a few, sad, last gray hairs,
  Where youth grows pale, and spectre-thin, and dies;
    Where but to think is to be full of sorrow
      And leaden-eyed despairs,
  Where Beauty cannot keep her lustrous eyes,
    Or new Love pine at them beyond to-morrow.

Away! away! for I will fly to thee,
  Not charioted by Bacchus and his pards,
But on the viewless wings of Poesy,
  Though the dull brain perplexes and retards:
Already with thee! tender is the night,
  And haply the Queen-Moon is on her throne,

Cluster'd around by all her starry Fays;
     But here there is no light,
Save what from heaven is with the breezes blown
     Through verdurous glooms and winding mossy ways.

I cannot see what flowers are at my feet,
     Nor what soft incense hangs upon the boughs,
But, in embalmed darkness, guess each sweet
     Wherewith the seasonable month endows
The grass, the thicket, and the fruit-tree wild;
     White hawthorn, and the pastoral eglantine;
          Fast fading violets cover'd up in leaves;
               And mid-May's eldest child,
     The coming musk-rose, full of dewy wine,
          The murmurous haunt of flies on summer eves.

Darkling I listen; and, for many a time
     I have been half in love with easeful Death,
Call'd him soft names in many a mused rhyme,
     To take into the air my quiet breath;
Now more than ever seems it rich to die,
     To cease upon the midnight with no pain,
          While thou art pouring forth thy soul abroad
               In such an ecstasy!
     Still wouldst thou sing, and I have ears in vain –
          To thy high requiem become a sod.

Thou wast not born for death, immortal Bird!
     No hungry generations tread thee down;
The voice I hear this passing night was heard
     In ancient days by emperor and clown:
Perhaps the self-same song that found a path
     Through the sad heart of Ruth, when, sick for home,
          She stood in tears amid the alien corn;
               The same that oft-times hath
     Charm'd magic casements, opening on the foam
          Of perilous seas, in faery lands forlorn.

Forlorn! the very word is like a bell
     To toll me back from thee to my sole self!
Adieu! the fancy cannot cheat so well
     As she is fam'd to do, deceiving elf.

Adieu! adieu! thy plaintive anthem fades
  Past the near meadows, over the still stream,
    Up the hill-side; and now 'tis buried deep
      In the next valley-glades:
  Was it a vision, or a waking dream?
    Fled is that music: – Do I wake or sleep?

JOHN KEATS

from The Odyssey (Book XVII)

Such speech they changed; when in the yard there lay
A dog, call'd Argus, which, before his way
Assumed for Ilion, Ulysses bred,
Yet stood his pleasure then in little stead,
As being too young, but, growing to his grace,
Young men made choice of him for every chace,
Or of their wild goats, of their hares, or harts.
But, his king gone, and he, now past his parts,
Lay all abjectly on the stable's store,
Before the ox-stall, and mules' stable door,
To keep the clothes cast from the peasants' hands,
While they laid compass on Ulysses' lands,
The dog, with ticks (unlook'd to) overgrown.
But by this dog no sooner seen but known
Was wise Ulysses, who new enter'd there,
Up went his dog's laid ears, and, coming near,
Up he himself rose, fawn'd, and wagg'd his stern,
Couch'd close his ears, and lay so; nor discern
Could evermore his dear-loved lord again.
Ulysses saw it, nor had power t' abstain
From shedding tears; which (far-off seeing his swain)
He dried from his sight clean; to whom he thus
His grief dissembled: ''Tis miraculous,
That such a dog as this should have his lair
On such a dunghill, for his form is fair.
And yet, I know not, if there were in him
Good pace, or parts, for all his goodly limb;

Or he lived empty of those inward things,
As are those trencher-beagles tending kings,
Whom for their pleasure's, or their glory's, sake,
Or fashion, they into their favours take.'
  'This dog,' said he, 'was servant to one dead
A huge time since. But if he bore his head,
For form and quality, of such a height,
As when Ulysses, bound for th'Ilion fight,
Or quickly after, left him, your rapt eyes
Would then admire to see him use his thighs
In strength and swiftness. He would nothing fly,
Nor anything let 'scape. If once his eye
Seized any wild beast, he knew straight his scent;
Go where he would, away with him he went.
Nor was there ever any savage stood
Amongst the thickets of the deepest wood
Long time before him, but he pull'd him down;
As well by that true hunting to be shown
In such vast coverts, as for speed of pace
In any open lawn. For in deep chace
He was a passing wise and well-nosed hound.
And yet is all this good in him uncrown'd
With any grace here now, nor he more fed
Than any errant cur. His king is dead,
Far from his country; and his servants are
So negligent they lend his hound no care.
Where masters rule not, but let men alone,
You never there see honest service done.
That man's half virtue Jove takes quite away,
That once is sun-burnt with the servile day.'

HOMER
Translated by George Chapman

Of the Pythagorean Philosophy

From Ovid's Metamorphoses, *Book XV*

'A race of men there are, as fame has told,
Who shivering suffer hyperborean cold,
Till nine times bathing in Minerva's lake,
Soft feathers, to defend their naked sides, they take.
'Tis said, the Scythian wives (believe who will)
Transform themselves to birds by magic skill;
Smeared over with an oil of wonderous might,
That adds new pinions to their airy flight.
    'But this by sure experiment we know
That living creatures from corruption grow:
Hide in a hollow pit a slaughtered steer,
Bees from his putrid bowels will appear;
Who like their parents haunt the fields, and bring
Their honey harvest home, and hope another spring.
The warlike steed is multiplied we find,
To wasps and hornets of the warrior kind.
Cut from a crab his crooked claws and hide
The rest in earth, a scorpion thence will glide
And shoot his sting, his tail in circles tossed
Refers the limbs his backward father lost.
And worms, that stretch on leaves their filmy loom,
Crawl from their bags, and butterflies become.
E'en slime begets the frog's loquacious race:
Short of their feet at first, in little space
With arms and legs endued, long leaps they take,
Raised on their hinder part, and swim the lake,
And waves repel: for nature gives their kind
To that intent, a length of legs behind.
    'The cubs of bears, a living lump appear,
When whelped, and no determined figure wear.
Their mother licks them into shape, and gives
As much of form, as she herself receives.
    'The grubs from their sexangular abode
Crawl out unfinished, like the maggot's brood,
Trunks without limbs; till time at leisure brings
The thighs they wanted, and their tardy wings.

'The bird who draws the car of Juno, vain
Of her crowned head, and of her starry train;
And he that bears the artillery of Jove,
The strong-pounced eagle, and the billing dove;
And all the feathered kind, who could suppose
(But that from sight, the surest sense he knows)
They from the included yolk, not ambient white, arose.

'There are who think the marrow of a man,
Which in the spine, while he was living, ran;
When dead, the pith corrupted will become
A snake, and hiss within the hollow tomb.

'All these receive their birth from other things;
But from himself the phoenix only springs:
Self-born, begotten by the parent flame
In which he burned, another and the same;
Who not by corn or herbs his life sustains,
But the sweet essence of amomum drains,
And watches the rich gums Arabia bears,
While yet in tender dew they drop their tears.
He (his five centuries of life fulfilled)
His nest on oaken boughs begins to build,
Or trembling tops of palm, and first he draws
The plan with his broad bill, and crooked claws,
Nature's artificers; on this the pile
Is formed, and rises round, then with the spoil
Of cassia, cinnamon, and stems of nard,
(For softness strewed beneath,) his funeral bed is reared:
Funeral and bridal both; and all around
The borders with corruptless myrrh are crowned,
On this incumbent; till etherial flame
First catches, then consumes the costly frame:
Consumes him too, as on the pile he lies;
He lived on odours, and in odours dies.

'An infant phoenix from the former springs
His father's heir, and from his tender wings
Shakes off his parent dust, his method he pursues,
And the same lease of life on the same terms renews.
When grown to manhood he begins his reign,
And with stiff pinions can his flight sustain,
He lightens of its load the tree that bore

His father's royal sepulchre before,
And his own cradle: (this with pious care
Placed on his back) he cuts the buxom air,
Seeks the sun's city, and his sacred church,
And decently lays down his burden in the porch.
   'A wonder more amazing would we find?
The hyena shows it, of a double kind,
Varying the sexes in alternate years,
In one begets, and in another bears.
The thin chameleon fed with air, receives
The colour of the thing to which he cleaves.
   'India when conquered, on the conquering god
For planted vines the sharp-eyed lynx bestowed,
Whose urine shed, before it touches earth,
Congeals in air, and gives to gems their birth.
So coral soft, and white in ocean's bed,
Comes hardened up in air, and glows with red.
   'All changing species should my song recite,
Before I ceased, would change the day to night.
Nations and empires flourish and decay,
By turns command, and in their turns obey;
Time softens hardy people, time again
Hardens to war a soft, unwarlike train.
Thus Troy for ten long years her foes withstood,
And daily bleeding bore the expense of blood;
Now for thick streets it shows an empty space,
Or only filled with tombs of her own perished race,
Herself becomes the sepulchre of what she was.

JOHN DRYDEN

On a Cock at Rochester

Thou cursed Cock, with thy perpetual Noise,
May'st thou be Capon made, and lose thy Voice,
Or on a Dunghil may'st thou spend thy Blood,
And Vermin prey upon thy craven Brood;
May Rivals tread thy Hens before thy Face,

Then with redoubled Courage give thee chase;
May'st thou be punish'd for St *Peter*'s Crime,
And on *Shrove-tuesday*, perish in thy Prime;
May thy bruis'd Carcass be some Beggar's Feast,
Thou first and worst Disturber of Man's Rest.

SIR CHARLES SEDLEY

On a Dog of Lord Eglinton's

I never barked when out of season,
    I never bit without a reason;
I ne'er insulted weaker brother,
    Nor wronged by force or fraud another.
We brutes are placed a rank below;
    Happy for man could he say so.

ROBERT BURNS

On Seeing a Wounded Hare Limp by Me, Which a Fellow had just Shot at

Inhuman man! curse on thy barb'rous art,
    And blasted be thy murder-aiming eye;
    May never pity soothe thee with a sigh,
Nor ever pleasure glad thy cruel heart!

Go live, poor wanderer of the wood and field,
    The bitter little that of life remains:
    No more the thickening brakes and verdant plains
To thee shall home, or food, or pastime yield.

Seek, mangled wretch, some place of wonted rest,
    No more of rest, but now thy dying bed!
    The sheltering rushes whistling o'er thy head,
The cold earth with thy bloody bosom prest.

Oft as by winding Nith I, musing, wait
  The sober eve, or hail the chearful dawn,
  I'll miss thee sporting o'er the dewy lawn,
And curse the ruffian's aim, and mourn thy hapless fate.

ROBERT BURNS

from Oppian's Halieuticks

Justly might Female *Tortoises* complain,
To whom Enjoyment is the greatest Pain.
They dread the Tryal, and foreboding hate
The growing Passion of the cruel Mate.
He amorous pursues, They conscious fly
Joyless Caresses, and resolv'd deny.
Since partial Heaven has thus restrain'd the Bliss,
The Males they welcome with a closer Kiss,
Bite angry, and reluctant Hate declare.
The *Tortoise-Courtship* is a State of War.
Eager they fight, but with unlike Design,
Males to obtain, and Females to decline.
The Conflict lasts, till these by Strength o'ercome
All sorrowing yield to the resistless Doom.
Not like a Bride, but pensive Captive, led
To the loath'd Duties of a hated Bed.

WILLIAM DIAPER

An Otter

I
  Underwater eyes, an eel's
Oil of water body, neither fish nor beast is the otter:
  Four-legged yet water-gifted, to outfish fish;
    With webbed feet and long ruddering tail
    And a round head like an old tomcat.

Brings the legend of himself
From before wars or burials, in spite of hounds and vermin-poles;
　　Does not take root like the badger. Wanders, cries;
　　　　Gallops along land he no longer belongs to;
　　　　Re-enters the water by melting.

　　　　Of neither water nor land. Seeking
Some world lost when first he dived, that he cannot come at since,
　　Takes his changed body into the holes of lakes;
　　　　As if blind, cleaves the stream's push till he licks
　　　　The pebbles of the source; from sea

　　　　To sea crosses in three nights
Like a king in hiding. Crying to the old shape of the starlit land,
　　Over sunken farms where the bats go round,
　　　　Without answer. Till light and birdsong come
　　　　Walloping up roads with the milk wagon.

2

The hunt's lost him. Pads on mud,
Among sedges, nostrils a surface bead,
The otter remains, hours. The air,
Circling the globe, tainted and necessary,

Mingling tobacco-smoke, hounds and parsley,
Comes carefully to the sunk lungs.
So the self under the eye lies,
Attendant and withdrawn. The otter belongs

In double robbery and concealment –
From water that nourishes and drowns, and from land
That gave him his length and the mouth of the hound.
He keeps fat in the limpid integument

Reflections live on. The heart beats thick,
Big trout muscle out of the dead cold;
Blood is the belly of logic; he will lick
The fishbone bare. And can take stolen hold

On a bitch otter in a field full
Of nervous horses, but linger nowhere.
Yanked above hounds, reverts to nothing at all,
To this long pelt over the back of a chair.

TED HUGHES

The Otter

When you plunged
The light of Tuscany wavered
And swung through the pool
From top to bottom.

I loved your wet head and smashing crawl,
Your fine swimmer's back and shoulders
Surfacing and surfacing again
This year and every year since.

I sat dry-throated on the warm stones.
You were beyond me.
The mellowed clarities, the grape-deep air
Thinned and disappointed.

Thank God for the slow loadening,
When I hold you now
We are close and deep
As the atmosphere on water.

My two hands are plumbed water.
You are my palpable, lithe
Otter of memory
In the pool of the moment,

Turning to swim on your back,
Each silent, thigh-shaking kick
Re-tilting the light,
Heaving the cool at your neck.

And suddenly you're out,
Back again, intent as ever,
Heavy and frisky in your freshened pelt,
Printing the stones.

SEAMUS HEANEY

'Our little Kinsmen – after Rain'

Our little Kinsmen – after Rain
In plenty may be seen,
A Pink and Pulpy multitude
The tepid Ground upon.

A needless life, it seemed to me
Until a little Bird
As to a Hospitality
Advanced and breakfasted.

As I of He, so God of Me
I pondered, may have judged,
And left the little Angle Worm
With Modesties enlarged.

EMILY DICKINSON

Out in the Dark

Out in the dark over the snow
The fallow fawns invisible go
With the fallow doe;
And the winds blow
Fast as the stars are slow.

Stealthily the dark haunts round
And, when the lamp goes, without sound

At a swifter bound
Than the swiftest hound,
Arrives, and all else is drowned;

And star and I and wind and deer
Are in the dark together, – near,
Yet far, – and fear
Drums on my ear
In that sage company drear.

How weak and little is the light,
All the universe of sight,
Love and delight,
Before the might,
If you love it not, of night.

EDWARD THOMAS

The Outlaw

Kelly's kept an unlicensed bull, well away
From the road: you risked fine but had to pay

The normal fee if cows were serviced there.
Once I dragged a nervous Friesian on a tether

Down a lane of alder, shaggy with catkin,
Down to the shed the bull was kept in.

I gave Old Kelly the clammy silver, though why
I could not guess. He grunted a curt 'Go by

Get up on that gate'. And from my lofty station
I watched the business-like conception.

The door, unbolted, whacked back against the wall.
The illegal sire fumbled from his stall

Unhurried as an old steam engine shunting.
He circled, snored and nosed. No hectic panting,

Just the unfussy ease of a good tradesman;
Then an awkward, unexpected jump, and

His knobbled forelegs straddling her flank,
He slammed life home, impassive as a tank,

Dropping off like a tipped-up load of sand.
'She'll do,' said Kelly and tapped his ash-plant

Across her hindquarters. 'If not, bring her back.'
I walked ahead of her, the rope now slack

While Kelly whooped and prodded his outlaw
Who, in his own time, resumed the dark, the straw.

SEAMUS HEANEY

The Owl and the Pussy-Cat

The Owl and the Pussy-cat went to sea
    In a beautiful pea-green boat,
They took some honey, and plenty of money,
    Wrapped up in a five-pound note.
The Owl looked up to the stars above,
    And sang to a small guitar,
'O lovely Pussy! O Pussy, my love,
    What a beautiful Pussy you are,
        You are,
        You are!
    What a beautiful Pussy you are!'

Pussy said to the Owl, 'You elegant fowl!
    How charmingly sweet you sing!
O let us be married! too long we have tarried:
    But what shall we do for a ring?'
They sailed away, for a year and a day,
    To the land where the Bong-tree grows
And there in a wood a Piggy-wig stood
    With a ring at the end of his nose,
        His nose,
        His nose,
    With a ring at the end of his nose.

'Dear Pig, are you willing to sell for one shilling
  Your ring?' Said the Piggy, 'I will.'
So they took it away, and were married next day
  By the Turkey who lives on the hill.
They dined on mince, and slices of quince,
  Which they ate with a runcible spoon;
And hand in hand, on the edge of the sand,
  They danced by the light of the moon,
      The moon,
      The moon,
  They danced by the light of the moon.

EDWARD LEAR

The Oxen

Christmas Eve, and twelve of the clock.
  'Now they are all on their knees,'
An elder said as we sat in a flock
  By the embers in hearthside ease.

We pictured the meek mild creatures where
  They dwelt in their strawy pen,
Nor did it occur to one of us there
  To doubt they were kneeling then.

So fair a fancy few would weave
  In these years! Yet, I feel,
If someone said on Christmas Eve,
  'Come; see the oxen kneel

'In the lonely barton by yonder coomb
  Our childhood used to know,'
I should go with him in the gloom,
  Hoping it might be so.

THOMAS HARDY

Parley of Beasts

Auld Noah was at hame wi' them a',
The lion and the lamb,
Pair by pair they entered the Ark
And he took them as they cam'.

If twa o' ilka beist there is
Into this room sud come,
Wad I cud welcome them like him,
And no' staun' gowpin' dumb!

Be chief wi' them and they wi' me
And a' wi' ane anither
As Noah and his couples were
There in the Ark thegither.

It's fain I'd mell wi' tiger and tit,
Wi' elephant and eel,
But noo-a-days e'en wi' ain's se
At hame it's hard to feel.

HUGH MACDIARMID

from The Parliament of Fowls

Whan I was come ayeyn into the place
That I of spak, that was so sote and grene,
Forth welk I tho' myselven to solace.
Tho was I war wher that ther sat a queene
That, as of lyght the somer sonne shene
Passeth the sterre, right so over mesure
She fayrer was than any creature.

And in a launde, upon an hil of floures,
Was set this noble goddesse Nature.
Of braunches were here halles and here boures
Iwrought after here cast and here mesure;
Ne there nas foul that cometh of engendrure
That they ne were prest in here presence,

To take hire dom and yeve hire audyence.

For this was on seynt Valentynes day,
Whan every foul cometh there to chese his make,
Of every kynde that men thynke may,
And that so huge a noyse gan they make
That erthe, and eyr, and tre, and every lake
So ful was, that unethe was there space
For me to stonde, so ful was al the place.

And right as Aleyn, in the Pleynt of Kynde,
Devyseth Nature of aray and face,
In swich aray men myghte hire there fynde.
This noble emperesse, ful of grace,
Bad every foul to take his owne place,
As they were woned alwey fro yer to yeere,
Seynt Valentynes day, to stonden theere.

That is to seyn, the foules of ravyne
Weere hyest set, and thanne the foules smale
That eten, as hem Nature wolde enclyne,
As worm or thyng of which I telle no tale;
And water-foul sat lowest in the dale;
But foul that lyveth by sed sat on the grene,
And that so fele that wonder was to sene.

There myghte men the royal egle fynde,
That with his sharpe lok perseth the sonne,
And othere egles of a lowere kynde,
Of whiche that clerkes wel devyse conne.
Ther was the tiraunt with his fetheres donne
And grey, I mene the goshauk, that doth pyne
To bryddes for his outrageous ravyne.

The gentyl faucoun, that with his feet distrayneth
The kynges hand; the hardy sperhauk eke,
The quayles foo; the merlioun, that payneth
Hymself ful ofte the larke for to seke;
There was the douve with hire yën meke;
The jelous swan, ayens his deth that syngeth;
The oule ek, that of deth the bode bryngeth;

The crane, the geaunt, with his trompes soun;
The thef, the chough; and ek the janglynge pye;
The skornynge jay; the eles fo, heroun;
The false lapwynge, ful of trecherye;
The stare, that the conseyl can bewrye;
The tame ruddok, and the coward kyte;
The kok, that orloge is of thorpes lyte;

The sparwe, Venus sone; the nyghtyngale,
That clepeth forth the grene leves newe;
The swalwe, mortherere of the foules smale
That maken hony of floures freshe of hewe;
The wedded turtil, with hire herte trewe;
The pekok, with his aungels fetheres bryghte;
The fesaunt, skornere of the cok by nyghte;

The waker goos; the cukkow ever unkynde;
The popynjay, ful of delicasye;
The drake, stroyere of his owene kynde;
The stork, the wrekere of avouterye;
The hote cormeraunt of glotenye;
The raven wys; the crowe with vois of care;
The throstil old; the frosty feldefare.

What shulde I seyn? Of foules every kynde
That in this world han fetheres and stature
Men myghten in that place assembled fynde
Byfore the noble goddesse of Nature,
And everich of hem dide his besy cure
Benygnely to chese or for to take,
By hire acord, his formel or his make.

GEOFFREY CHAUCER

The Partridge

One day accross the fields I chancd to pass
When chickens chelped and skuttled in the grass
And as I looked about to find the seat
A wounded partridge dropped agen my feet

She fluttered round and calling as she lay
The chickens chelpd and fluttered all away
I stooped to pick her up when up she drew
Her wounded wing and cackled as she flew
I wondered much to hear the chickens lye
As still as nothing till I wandered bye
And soon she came agen with much ado
And swept the grass and called them as she flew
But still they kept their seat and left no trace
And old cows snorted when they passed the place

JOHN CLARE

The Phoenix and the Turtle

Let the bird of loudest lay
On the sole Arabian tree
Herald sad and trumpet be,
To whose sound chaste wings obey.

But thou shrieking harbinger,
Foul precurrer of the fiend,
Augur of the fever's end,
To this troop come thou not near.

From this session interdict
Every fowl of tyrant wing,
Save the eagle, feath'red king:
Keep the obsequy so strict.

Let the priest in surplice white,
That defunctive music can,
Be the death-divining swan,
Lest the requiem lack his right.

And thou treble-dated crow,
That thy sable gender mak'st
With the breath thou giv'st and tak'st,
'Mongst our mourners shalt thou go.

Here the anthem doth commence:
Love and constancy is dead,
Phoenix and the turtle fled
In a mutual flame from hence.

So they loved, as love in twain
Had the essence but in one;
Two distincts, division none:
Number there in love was slain.

Hearts remote, yet not asunder;
Distance and no space was seen
'Twixt this turtle and his queen;
But in them it were a wonder.

So between them love did shine
That the turtle saw his right
Flaming in the phoenix' sight:
Either was the other's mine.

Property was thus appallèd,
That the self was not the same;
Single nature's double name
Neither two nor one was callèd.

Reason, in itself confounded,
Saw division grow together,
To themselves yet either neither,
Simple were so well compounded;

That it cried, 'How true a twain
Seemeth this concordant one!
Love hath reason, reason none,
If what parts can so remain.'

Whereupon it made this threne
To the phoenix and the dove,
Co-supremes and stars of love,
As chorus to their tragic scene.

THRENOS

Beauty, truth, and rarity,
Grace in all simplicity,
Here enclosed, in cinders lie.

Death is now the phoenix' nest,
And the turtle's loyal breast
To eternity doth rest,

Leaving no posterity:
'Twas not their infirmity,
It was married chastity.

Truth may seem, but cannot be;
Beauty brag, but 'tis not she:
Truth and Beauty buried be.

To this urn let those repair
That are either true or fair;
For these dead birds sigh a prayer.

WILLIAM SHAKESPEARE

Pied Beauty

Glory be to God for dappled things –
 For skies of couple-colour as a brinded cow;
  For rose-moles all in stipple upon trout that swim;
Fresh-firecoal chestnut-falls; finches' wings;
 Landscape plotted and pieced – fold, fallow, and plough;
  And áll trádes, their gear and tackle and trim.
All things counter, original, spare, strange;
 Whatever is fickle, freckled (who knows how?)
  With swift, slow; sweet, sour; adazzle, dim;
He fathers-forth whose beauty is past change:
      Praise him.

GERARD MANLEY HOPKINS

from The Pied Piper of Hamelin

A Child's Story

Hamelin Town's in Brunswick,
   By famous Hanover city;
The river Weser, deep and wide,
Washes its wall on the southern side;
A pleasanter spot you never spied;
   But, when begins my ditty,
Almost five hundred years ago,
To see the townsfolk suffer so
   From vermin, was a pity.

   Rats!
They fought the dogs and killed the cats,
   And bit the babies in the cradles,
And ate the cheeses out of the vats,
   And licked the soup from the cooks' own ladles,
Split open the kegs of salted sprats,
Made nests inside men's Sunday hats,
And even spoiled the women's chats
     By drowning their speaking
     With shrieking and squeaking
In fifty different sharps and flats.

At last the people in a body
   To the Town Hall came flocking:
'Tis clear,' cried they, 'our Mayor's a noddy;
   And as for our Corporation – shocking
To think we buy gowns lined with ermine
For dolts that can't or won't determine
What's best to rid us of our vermin!
You hope, because you're old and obese,
To find in the furry civic robe ease?
Rouse up, sirs! Give your brains a racking
To find the remedy we're lacking,
Or, sure as fate, we'll send you packing!'
At this the Mayor and Corporation
Quaked with a mighty consternation.

An hour they sat in council,
　At length the Mayor broke silence:
'For a guilder I'd my ermine gown sell,
　I wish I were a mile hence!
It's easy to bid one rack one's brain –
I'm sure my poor head aches again,
I've scratched it so, and all in vain.
Oh for a trap, a trap, a trap!'
Just as he said this, what should hap
At the chamber door but a gentle tap?
'Bless us,' cried the Mayor, 'what's that?'
(With the Corporation as he sat,
Looking little though wondrous fat;
Nor brighter was his eye, nor moister
Than a too-long-opened oyster,
Save when at noon his paunch grew mutinous
For a plate of turtle green and glutinous)
'Only a scraping of shoes on the mat?
Anything like the sound of a rat
Makes my heart go pit-a-pat!'

'Come in!' – the Mayor cried, looking bigger.
And in did come the strangest figure!
His queer long coat from heel to head
Was half of yellow and half of red,
And he himself was tall and thin,
With sharp blue eyes, each like a pin,
And light loose hair, yet swarthy skin,
No tuft on cheek nor beard on chin,
But lips where smiles went out and in;
There was no guessing his kith and kin:
And nobody could enough admire
The tall man and his quaint attire.
Quoth one: 'It's as my great-grandsire,
Starting up at the Trump of Doom's tone,
Had walked this way from his painted tombstone!'

He advanced to the council-table:
And, 'Please your honours,' said he, I'm able,
By means of a secret charm, to draw
   All creatures living beneath the sun,
   That creep or swim or fly or run,
After me so as you never saw!
And I chiefly use my charm
On creatures that do people harm,
The mole and toad and newt and viper;
And people call me the Pied Piper.'
(And here they noticed round his neck
   A scarf of red and yellow stripe,
To match with his coat of the self-same cheque;
   And at the scarf's end hung a pipe;
And his fingers, they noticed, were ever straying
As if impatient to be playing
Upon this pipe, as low it dangled
Over his vesture so old-fangled.)
'Yet,' said he, 'poor piper as I am,
In Tartary I freed the Cham,
   Last June, from his huge swarms of gnats;
I eased in Asia the Nizam
   Of a monstrous brood of vampyre-bats:
And as for what your brain bewilders,
   If I can rid your town of rats
Will you give me a thousand guilders?'
'One? fifty thousand!' – was the exclamation
Of the astonished Mayor and Corporation.

Into the street the Piper stept,
   Smiling first a little smile,
As if he knew what magic slept
   In his quiet pipe the while;
Then, like a musical adept,
To blow the pipe his lips he wrinkled,
And green and blue his sharp eyes twinkled,
Like a candle-flame where salt is sprinkled;
And ere three shrill notes the pipe uttered,
You heard as if an army muttered;
And the muttering grew to a grumbling;

And the grumbling grew to a mighty rumbling;
And out of the houses the rats came tumbling.
Great rats, small rats, lean rats, brawny rats,
Brown rats, black rats, grey rats, tawny rats,
Grave old plodders, gay young friskers,
   Fathers, mothers, uncles, cousins,
Cocking tails and pricking whiskers,
   Families by tens and dozens,
Brothers, sisters, husbands, wives –
Followed the Piper for their lives.
From street to street he piped advancing,
And step for step they followed dancing,
Until they came to the river Weser,
   Wherein all plunged and perished!
– Save one who, stout as Julius Caesar,
Swam across and lived to carry
   (As he, the manuscript he cherished)
To Rat-land home his commentary:
Which was, 'At the first shrill notes of the pipe,
I heard a sound as of scraping tripe,
And putting apples, wondrous ripe,
Into a cider-press's gripe:
And a moving away of pickle-tub-boards,
And a leaving ajar of conserve-cupboards,
And a drawing the corks of train-oil-flasks,
And a breaking the hoops of butter-casks:
And it seemed as if a voice
   (Sweeter far than by harp or by psaltery
Is breathed) called out, "Oh rats, rejoice!
   The world is grown to one vast drysaltery!
So munch on, crunch on, take your nuncheon,
Breakfast, supper, dinner, luncheon!"
And just as a bulky sugar-puncheon,
All ready staved, like a great sun shone
Glorious scarce an inch before me,
Just as methought it said, "Come, bore me!"
– I found the Weser rolling o'er me.'

ROBERT BROWNING

Pigs

Us all on sore cement was we.
Not warmed then with glares. Not glutting mush
under that pole the lightning's tied to.
No farrow-shit in milk to make us randy.
Us back in cool god-shit. We ate crisp.
We nosed up good rank in the tunnelled bush.
Us all fuckers then. And Big, huh? Tusked
the balls-biting dog and gutsed him wet.
Us shoved down the soft cement of rivers.
Us snored the earth hollow, filled farrow, grunted.
Never stopped growing. We sloughed, we soughed
and balked no weird till the high ridgebacks was us
with weight-buried hooves. Or bristly, with milk.
Us never knowed like slitting nor hose-biff then.
Not the terrible sheet-cutting screams up ahead.
The burnt water kicking. This gone-already feeling
here in no place with our heads on upside down.

LES MURRAY

Pike

Pike, three inches long, perfect
Pike in all parts, green tigering the gold.
Killers from the egg: the malevolent aged grin.
They dance on the surface among the flies.

Or move, stunned by their own grandeur,
Over a bed of emerald, silhouette
Of submarine delicacy and horror.
A hundred feet long in their world.

In ponds, under the heat-struck lily pads –
Gloom of their stillness:
Logged on last year's black leaves, watching upwards.
Or hung in an amber cavern of weeds

The jaws' hooked clamp and fangs
Not to be changed at this date;
A life subdued to its instrument;
The gills kneading quietly, and the pectorals.

Three we kept behind glass,
Jungled in weed: three inches, four,
And four and a half: fed fry to them –
Suddenly there were two. Finally one

With a sag belly and the grin it was born with.
And indeed they spare nobody.
Two, six pounds each, over two feet long,
High and dry and dead in the willow-herb –

One jammed past its gills down the other's gullet:
The outside eye stared: as a vice locks –
The same iron in this eye
Though its film shrank in death.

A pond I fished, fifty yards across,
Whose lilies and muscular tench
Had outlasted every visible stone
Of the monastery that planted them –

Stilled legendary depth:
It was as deep as England. It held
Pike too immense to stir, so immense and old
That past nightfall I dared not cast

But silently cast and fished
With the hair frozen on my head
For what might move, for what eye might move.
The still splashes on the dark pond,

Owls hushing the floating woods
Frail on my ear against the dream
Darkness beneath night's darkness had freed,
That rose slowly towards me, watching.

TED HUGHES

The Polar Bear

his coat resembles the snow
deep snow
the male snow
which attacks and kills

silently as it falls muffling
the world
to sleep that
the interrupted quiet return

to lie down with us
its arms
about our necks
murderously a little while

WILLIAM CARLOS WILLIAMS

Pretty Baa Lamb

On tiptoe over to my baby daughter,
the umbilicus a black twig,

thin as a strand of spaghetti,
caught in the fleece.

It balances on thick joints
like an old woman's fingers –

bones in a liberty bodice
the colour of ash,

a tight garment
bouclé with crisp cinders.

I give it a finger to suck
and it pulls like a plughole

with the fierce strength
of a week, while I notice

orange rubber bands around
the scrotum and the tail –

they will wither, unnoticed
as the brittle umbilicus.

Its life a death
exact in every detail,

the lamb belongs here
in the improbable dream

we tell to each other,
day after day, before it fades.

CRAIG RAINE

The Pride of Youth

Proud Maisie is in the wood,
  Walking so early;
Sweet Robin sits on the bush
  Singing so rarely.

'Tell me, thou bonny bird,
  When shall I marry me?'
'When six braw gentlemen
  Kirkward shall carry ye.'

'Who makes the bridal bed,
  Birdie, say truly?'
'The grey-headed sexton
  That delves the grave duly.

'The glow-worm o'er grave and stone
    Shall light thee steady;
The owl from the steeple sing
    Welcome, proud lady.'

SIR WALTER SCOTT

A Rabbit as King of the Ghosts

The difficulty to think at the end of day,
When the shapeless shadow covers the sun
And nothing is left except light on your fur –

There was the cat slopping its milk all day,
Fat cat, red tongue, green mind, white milk
And August the most peaceful month.

To be, in the grass, in the peacefullest time,
Without that monument of cat,
The cat forgotten in the moon;

And to feel that the light is a rabbit-light,
In which everything is meant for you
And nothing need be explained;

Then there is nothing to think of. It comes of itself;
And east rushes west and west rushes down,
No matter. The grass is full

And full of yourself. The trees around are for you,
The whole of the wideness of night is for you,
A self that touches all edges,

You become a self that fills the four corners of night.
The red cat hides away in the fur-light
And there you are humped high, humped up,

You are humped higher and higher, black as stone –
You sit with your head like a carving in space
And the little green cat is a bug in the grass.

WALLACE STEVENS

'Repeat that, repeat'

Repeat that, repeat,
Cuckoo, bird, and open ear wells, heart-springs, delightfully sweet,
With a ballad, with a ballad, a rebound
Off trundled timber and scoops of the hillside ground, hollow hollow
    hollow ground:
The whole landscape flushes on a sudden at a sound.

    GERARD MANLEY HOPKINS

Riddles from *The Exeter Book*

Silent is my dress when I step across the earth,
reside in my house, or ruffle the waters.
Sometimes my adornments and this high windy air
lift me over the livings of men,
the power of the clouds carries me far
over all people. My white pinions
resound very loudly, ring with a melody,
sing out clearly, when I sleep not on
the soil or settle on grey waters – a travelling spirit.

        *

In former days my mother and father
forsook me for dead, for the fullness of life
was not yet within me. But a kinswoman
graciously fitted me out in soft garments,
as kind to me as to her own children,
tended and took me under her wing;
until under shelter, unlike her kin,
I matured as a mighty bird (as was my fate).
My guardian then fed me until I could fly
and wander more widely on my
excursions; she had the less of her own
sons and daughters by what she did thus.

My beak was bound and I was immersed,
the current swept round me as I lay covered
by mountain streams; I matured in the sea,
above the milling waves, my body
locked to a stray, floating spar.
When, in black garments, I left wave
and wood, I was full of life;
some of my clothing was white
when the tides of air lifted me,
the wind from the wave, then carried me far
over the seal's bath. Say what I am called.

*

I saw a creature: masculine, greedy
with all youth's abandon. As his due
his guardian gave him four springs,
four fountains, shooting and shining.
A man spoke, he said to me:
'Alive, that creature breaks the downs;
dead and shredded, he binds the living.'

*

A moth devoured words. When I heard
of that wonder it struck me as a strange event
that a worm should swallow the song of some man,
a thief gorge in the darkness on fine phrases
and their firm foundation. The thievish stranger
was not a whit the wiser for swallowing words.

*

Sea suckled me, waves sounded over me,
rollers covered me as I rested on my bed.
I have no feet and often open my mouth
to the flood. Now some man will
consume me, who cares nothing for my clothing.

With the point of his knife he will rip the skin
away from my side, and straight away eat me
uncooked as I am . . .

ANONYMOUS
Translated from the Old English by Kevin Crossley-Holland

The Ride

The horse beneath me seemed
To know what course to steer
Through the horror of snow I dreamed,
And so I had no fear,

Nor was I chilled to death
By the wind's white shudders, thanks
To the veils of his patient breath
And the mist of sweat from his flanks.

It seemed that all night through,
Within my hand no rein
And nothing in my view
But the pillar of his mane,

I rode with magic ease
At a quick, unstumbling trot
Through shattering vacancies
On into what was not,

Till the weave of the storm grew thin,
With a threading of cedar-smoke,
And the ice-blind pane of an inn
Shimmered, and I awoke.

How shall I now get back
To the inn-yard where he stands,
Burdened with every lack,
And waken the stable-hands

To give him, before I think

That there was no horse at all,
Some hay, some water to drink,
A blanket and a stall?

RICHARD WILBUR

Ride a Cock-Horse

Ride a cock-horse to Banbury Cross,
To see a fine lady upon a white horse;
Rings on her fingers and bells on her toes,
She shall have music wherever she goes.

ANONYMOUS

from The Rime of the Ancient Mariner

An ancient Mariner
meeteth three gallants
bidden to a wedding-
feast, and detaineth
one.

It is an ancient Mariner,
And he stoppeth one of three.
'By thy long grey beard and glittering eye,
Now wherefore stopp'st thou me?

The Bridegroom's doors are opened wide,
And I am next of kin;
The guests are met, the feast is set:
May'st hear the merry din.'

He holds him with his skinny hand,
'There was a ship,' quoth he.
'Hold off! unhand me, grey-beard loon!'
Eftsoons his hand dropt he.

The wedding guest is
spellbound by the eye
of the old seafaring
man, and constrained
to hear his tale.

He holds him with his glittering eye –
The wedding-guest stood still,
And listens like a three years' child:
The Mariner hath his will.

The wedding-guest sat on a stone:

He cannot choose but hear;
And thus spake on that ancient man,
The bright-eyed Mariner.

'The ship was cheered, the harbour cleared,
Merrily did we drop
Below the kirk, below the hill,
Below the lighthouse top.

The Mariner tells how
the ship sailed
southward with a
good wind and fair
weather, till it reached
the line.

The sun came up upon the left,
Out of the sea came he!
And he shone bright, and on the right
Went down into the sea.

Higher and higher every day,
Till over the mast at noon – '
The Wedding-Guest here beat his breast,
For he heard the loud bassoon.

The wedding guest
heareth the bridal
music; but the
mariner continueth
his tale.

The bride hath paced into the hall,
Red as a rose is she;
Nodding their heads before her goes
The merry minstrelsy.

The Wedding-Guest he beat his breast,
Yet he cannot choose but hear;
And thus spake on that ancient man,
The bright-eyed Mariner.

The ship drawn by a
storm toward the
south pole.

And now the storm-blast came, and he
Was tyrannous and strong:
He struck with his o'ertaking wings,
And chased us south along.

With sloping masts and dipping prow,
As who pursued with yell and blow
Still treads the shadow of his foe,
And foward bends his head,
The ship drove fast, loud roared the blast,
And southward aye we fled.

And now there came both mist and snow,
And it grew wondrous cold:
And ice, mast-high, came floating by,
As green as emerald.

The land of ice, and of fearful sounds where no living thing was to be seen.

And through the drifts the snowy clifts
Did send a dismal sheen:
Nor shapes of men nor beasts we ken –
The ice was all between.

The ice was here, the ice was there,
The ice was all around:
It cracked and growled, and roared and
    howled,
Like noises in a swound!

Till a great sea-bird, called the Albatross, came through the snow-fog, and was received with great joy and hospitality.

At length did cross an Albatross,
Thorough the fog it came;
As if it had been a Christian soul,
We hailed it in God's name.

It ate the food it ne'er had eat,
And round and round it flew.
The ice did split with a thunder-fit;
The helmsman steered us through!

And lo! the Albatross proveth a bird of good omen, and followeth the ship as it returned northward through fog and floating ice.

And a good south wind sprung up behind;
The Albatross did follow,
And every day, for food or play,
Came to the mariner's hollo!

In mist or cloud, on mast or shroud,
It perched for vespers nine;
Whiles all the night, through fog-smoke
    white,
Glimmered the white moon-shine.

The ancient Mariner inhospitably killeth the pious bird of good omen.

'God save thee, ancient Mariner!
From the fiends, that plague thee thus! –
Why look'st thou so?' – With my cross-bow
I shot the Albatross.

SAMUEL TAYLOR COLERIDGE

Robin, Wren, Martin, Swallow

The robin and the wren
Are God Almighty's cock and hen.
The martin and the swallow
Are God Almighty's bow and arrow.

ANONYMOUS

A Rum Cove, a Stout Cove

On the Barrack Islands far out
in the South Atlantic
the great-great-grandson (Sol Grout)
of Nelson's last bosun
is packing crawfish into a thick
barnacled keepbox marked *Briton
Kanning Factors Illimitated.*
It's his swart locks and cochin cheeks
that glim in the top left-hand corner
of 'Bold Bessie', the prime banner
that longs to LOL 301.
Like Gib, like the god called M'Lud,
and those tars behind locked doors
whistling *Britannia Rules*
in their slow skrimshandering
with worn and corded tools,
he's firm, Sol Grout, to the core,
the genius of these used islands
where no maritime elegists sing
of Resolution or Independence
with their harbourmaster's stores,
clagged mountains of ashy shale
and a small bird that noone has named –
a flightless timorous landrail
whose cry is rusted, hard, like chains.

TOM PAULIN

A Runnable Stag

When the pods went pop on the broom, green broom,
  And apples began to be golden-skinned,
We harboured a stag in the Priory coomb,
  And we feathered his trail up-wind, up-wind,
  We feathered his trail up-wind –
    A stag of warrant, a stag, a stag,
    A runnable stag, a kingly crop,
    Brow, bay and tray and three on top,
    A stag, a runnable stag.

Then the huntsman's horn rang yap, yap, yap,
  And 'Forwards' we heard the harbourer shout;
But 'twas only a brocket that broke a gap
  In the beechen underwood, driven out,
  From the underwood antlered out
    By warrant and might of the stag, the stag,
    The runnable stag, whose lordly mind
    Was bent on sleep, though beamed and tined
    He stood, a runnable stag.

So we tufted the covert till afternoon
  With Tinkerman's Pup and Bell-of-the-North;
And hunters were sulky and hounds out of tune
  Before we tufted the right stag forth,
  Before we tufted him forth,
    The stag of warrant, the wily stag,
    The runnable stag with his kingly crop,
    Brow, bay and tray and three on top,
    The royal and runnable stag.

It was Bell-of-the-North and Tinkerman's Pup
  That stuck to the scent till the copse was drawn.
'Tally ho! tally ho!' and the hunt was up,
  The tufters whipped and the pack laid on,
  The resolute pack laid on,
    And the stag of warrant away at last,
    The runnable stag, the same, the same,
    His hoofs on fire, his horns like flame,
    A stag, a runnable stag.

'Let your gelding be: if you check or chide
    He stumbles at once and you're out of the hunt;
For three hundred gentlemen, able to ride,
    On hunters accustomed to bear the brunt,
    Accustomed to bear the brunt,
        Are after the runnable stag, the stag,
        The runnable stag with his kingly crop,
        Brow, bay and tray and three on top,
        The right, the runnable stag.'

By perilous paths in coomb and dell,
    The heather, the rocks, and the river-bed,
The pace grew hot, for the scent lay well,
    And a runnable stag goes right ahead,
    The quarry went right ahead –
        Ahead, ahead, and fast and far;
        His antlered crest, his cloven hoof,
        Brow, bay and tray and three aloof,
        The stag, the runnable stag.

For a matter of twenty miles and more,
    By the densest hedge and the highest wall,
Through herds of bullocks he baffled the lore
    Of harbourer, huntsmen, hounds and all,
    Of harbourer, hounds and all –
        The stag of warrant, the wily stag,
        For twenty miles, and five and five,
        He ran, and he never was caught alive,
        This stag, this runnable stag.

When he turned at bay in the leafy gloom,
    In the emerald gloom where the brook ran deep,
He heard in the distance the rollers boom,
    And he saw in a vision of peaceful sleep,
    In a wonderful vision of sleep,
        A stag of warrant, a stag, a stag,
        A runnable stag in a jewelled bed,
        Under the sheltering ocean dead,
        A stag, a runnable stag.

So a fateful hope lit up his eye,
    And he opened his nostrils wide again,

And he tossed his branching antlers high
    As he headed the hunt down Charlock glen,
    As he raced down the echoing glen
        For five miles more, the stag, the stag,
        For twenty miles, and five and five,
        Not to be caught now, dead or alive,
        The stag, the runnable stag.

Three hundred gentlemen, able to ride,
    Three hundred horses as gallant and free,
Beheld him escape on the evening tide,
    Far out till he sank in the Severn Sea,
    Till he sank in the depths of the sea –
        The stag, the buoyant stag, the stag
        That slept at last in a jewelled bed
        Under the sheltering ocean spread,
        The stag, the runnable stag.

JOHN DAVIDSON

Saint Francis and the Sow

The bud
stands for all things,
even for those things that don't flower,
for everything flowers, from within, of self-blessing;
though sometimes it is necessary
to reteach a thing its loveliness,
to put a hand on its brow
of the flower
and retell it in words and in touch
it is lovely
until it flowers again from within, of self-blessing;
as Saint Francis
put his hand on the creased forehead
of the sow, and told her in words and in touch
blessings of earth on the sow, and the sow
began remembering all down her thick length,

from the earthen snout all the way
through the fodder and slops to the spiritual curl of the tail,
from the hard spininess spiked out from the spine
down through the great broken heart
to the sheer blue milken dreaminess spurting and shuddering
from the fourteen teats into the fourteen mouths sucking and blowing
   beneath them:
the long, perfect loveliness of sow.

GALWAY KINNELL

from The Seasons

SPRING
   When first the soul of love is sent abroad
Warm through the vital air, and on the heart
Harmonious seizes, the gay troops begin
In gallant thought to plume the painted wing;
And try again the long-forgotten strain,
At first aint-warbled. But no sooner grows
The soft infusion prevalent and wide
Than all alive at once their joy o'erflows
In music unconfined. Up springs the lark,
Shrill-voiced and loud, the messenger of morn:
Ere yet the shadows fly, he mounted sings
Amid the dawning clouds, and from their haunts
Calls up the tuneful nations. Every copse
Deep-tanged, tree irregular, and bush
Bending with dewy moisture o'er the heads
Of the coy quiristers that lodge within,
Are prodigal of harmony. The thrush
And wood-lark, o'er the kind-contending throng
Superior heard, run through the sweetest length
Of notes, when listening Philomela deigns
To let them joy, and purposes, in thought
Elate, to make her night excel their day.
The blackbird whistles from the thorny brake,
The mellow bullfinch answers from the grove;

Nor are the linnets, o'er the flowering furze
Poured out profusely, silent. Joined to these
Innumerous songsters, in the freshening shade
Of new-sprung leaves, their modulations mix
Mellifluous. The jay, the rook, the daw,
And each harsh pipe, discordant heard alone,
Aid the full concert; while the stock-dove breathes
A melancholy murmur through the whole.
   'Tis love creates their melody, and all
This waste of music is the voice of love,
That even to birds and beasts the tender arts
Of pleasing teaches. Hence the glossy kind
Try every winning way inventive love
Can dictate, and in courtship to their mates
Pour forth their little souls. First, wide around,
With distant awe, in airy rings they rove,
Endeavouring by a thousand tricks to catch
The cunning, conscious, half-averted glance
Of their regardless charmer. Should she seem
Softening the least approvance to bestow,
Their colours burnish, and, by hope inspired,
They brisk advance; then, on a sudden struck,
Retire disordered; then again approach,
In fond rotation spread the spotted wing,
And shiver every feather with desire.

AUTUMN
   Here the rude clamour of the sportsman's joy,
The gun fast-thundering and the winded horn,
Would tempt the Muse to sing the rural game, –
How, in his mid career, the spaniel, struck
Stiff by the tainted gale, with open nose
Outstretched and finely sensible, draws full,
Fearful, and cautious on the latent prey
As in the sun the circling covey bask
Their varied plumes, and, watchful every way,
Through the rough stubble turn the secret eye.
Caught in the meshy snare, in vain they beat
Their idle wings, entangled more and more:
Nor, on the surges of the boundless air

Though borne triumphant, are they safe; the gun,
Glanced just, and sudden, from the fowler's eye,
O'ertakes their sounding pinions, and again
Immediate brings them from the towering wing
Dead to the ground; or drives them wide-dispersed,
Wounded and wheeling various down the wind.
   These are not subjects for the peaceful muse,
Nor will she stain with such her spotless song –
Then most delighted when she social sees
The whole mixed animal creation round
Alive and happy. 'Tis not joy to her,
This falsely cheerful barbarous game of death,
This rage of pleasure which the restless youth
Awakes, impatient, with the gleaming morn;
When beasts of prey retire that all night long,
Urged by necessity, had ranged the dark,
As if their conscious ravage shunned the light
Ashamed. Not so the steady tyrant, man,
Who, with the thoughtless insolence of power
Inflamed beyond the most infuriate wrath
Of the worst monster that e'er roamed the waste,
For sport alone pursues the cruel chase
Amid the beamings of the gentle days.
Upbraid, ye ravening tribes, our wanton rage,
For hunger kindles you, and lawless want;
But lavish fed, in Nature's bounty rolled,
To joy at anguish, and delight in blood,
Is what your horrid bosoms never knew.
   Poor is the triumph o'er the timid hare!
Scared from the corn, and now to some lone seat
Retired – the rushy fen, the ragged furze
Stretched o'er the stony heath, the stubble chapped,
The thistly lawn, the thick entangled broom,
Of the same friendly hue the withered fern,
The fallow ground laid open to the sun
Concoctive, and the nodding sandy bank
Hung o'er the mazes of the mountain brook.
Vain is her best precaution; though she sits
Concealed with folded ears, unsleeping eyes
By Nature raised to take the horizon in,

And head couched close betwixt her hairy feet
In act to spring away. The scented dew
Betrays her early labyrinth; and deep,
In scattered sullen openings, far behind,
With every breeze she hears the coming storm
But, nearer and more frequent as it loads
The sighing gale, she springs amazed, and all
The savage soul of game is up at once –
The pack full-opening various, the shrill horn
Resounded from the hills, the neighing steed
Wild for the chase, and the loud hunter's shout –
O'er a weak, harmless, flying creature, all
Mixed in mad tumult and discordant joy.

   The stag, too, singled from the herd, where long
He ranged the branching monarch of the shades,
Before the tempest drives. At first, in speed
He sprightly puts his faith, and, roused by fear,
Gives all his swift aerial soul to flight.
Against the breeze he darts, that way the more
To leave the lessening murderous cry behind.
Deception short! though, fleeter than the winds
Blown o'er the keen-aired mountain by the North,
He bursts the thickets, glances through the glades,
And plunges deep into the wildest wood.
If slow, yet sure, adhesive to the track
Hot-steaming, up behind him come again
The inhuman rout, and from the shady depth
Expel him, circling through his every shift.
He sweeps the forest oft; and sobbing sees
The glades, mild opening to the golden day,
Where in kind contest with his butting friends
He wont to struggle, or his loves enjoy.
Oft in the full-descending flood he tries
To lose the scent, and lave his burning sides –
Oft seeks the herd; the watchful herd, alarmed,
With selfish care avoid a brother's woe.
What shall he do? His once so vivid nerves,
So full of buoyant spirit, now no more
Inspire the course; but fainting, breathless toil
Sick seizes on his heart: he stands at bay,

And puts his last weak refuge in despair.
The big round tears run down his dappled face;
He groans in anguish; while the growling pack,
Blood-happy, hang at his fair jutting chest,
And mark his beauteous chequered sides with gore.

JAMES THOMSON

The Silver Swan

The silver swan, who living had no note,
When death approached, unlocked her silent throat;
Leaning her breast against the reedy shore,
Thus sung her first and last, and sung no more:
'Farewell, all joys; Oh death, come close mine eyes;
More geese than swans now live, more fools than wise.'

ANONYMOUS

Sing a Song of Sixpence

Sing a song of sixpence,
  A pocket full of rye;
Four-and-twenty blackbirds,
  Baked in a pie.

When the pie was opened,
  The birds began to sing;
Was not that a dainty dish,
  To set before the king?

The king was in his counting-house,
  Counting out his money;
The queen was in the parlor
  Eating bread and honey.

The maid was in the garden,
   Hanging out the clothes,
When down came a blackbird
   And pecked off her nose.

ANONYMOUS

The Skunk

Up, black, striped and damasked like the chasuble
At a funeral mass, the skunk's tail
Paraded the skunk. Night after night
I expected her like a visitor.

The refrigerator whinnied into silence.
My desk light softened beyond the verandah.
Small oranges loomed in the orange tree.
I began to be tense as a voyeur.

After eleven years I was composing
Love-letters again, broaching the word 'wife'
Like a stored cask, as if its slender vowel
Had mutated into the night earth and air

Of California. The beautiful, useless
Tang of eucalyptus spelt your absence.
The aftermath of a mouthful of wine
Was like inhaling you off a cold pillow.

And there she was, the intent and glamorous,
Ordinary, mysterious skunk,
Mythologized, demythologized,
Snuffing the boards five feet beyond me.

It all came back to me last night, stirred
By the sootfall of your things at bedtime,
Your head-down, tail-up hunt in a bottom drawer
For the black plunge-line nightdress.

SEAMUS HEANEY

Skunk Hour

For Elizabeth Bishop

Nautilus Island's hermit
heiress still lives through winter in her Spartan cottage;
her sheep still graze above the sea.
Her son's a bishop. Her farmer
is first selectman in our village;
she's in her dotage.

Thirsting for
the hierarchic privacy
of Queen Victoria's century,
she buys up all
the eyesores facing her shore,
and lets them fall.

The season's ill –
we've lost our summer millionaire,
who seemed to leap from an L. L. Bean
catalogue. His nine-knot yawl
was auctioned off to lobstermen.
A red fox stain covers Blue Hill.

And now our fairy
decorator brightens his shop for fall;
his fishnet's filled with orange cork,
orange, his cobbler's bench and awl;
there is no money in his work,
he'd rather marry.

One dark night,
my Tudor Ford climbed the hill's skull;
I watched for love-cars. Lights turned down,
they lay together, hull to hull,
where the graveyard shelves on the town. . . .
My mind's not right.

A car radio bleats,
'Love, O careless Love. . . .' I hear
my ill-spirit sob in each blood cell,

as if my hand were at its throat. . . .
I myself am hell;
nobody's here –

only skunks, that search
in the moonlight for a bite to eat.
They march on their soles up Main Street:
white stripes, moonstruck eyes' red fire
under the chalk-dry and spar spire
of the Trinitarian Church.

I stand on top
of our back steps and breathe the rich air –
a mother skunk with her column of kittens swills the garbage pail.
She jabs her wedge-head in a cup
of sour cream, drops her ostrich tail,
and will not scare.

ROBERT LOWELL

The Sky Lark

The rolls and harrows lies at rest beside
The battered road and spreading far and wide
Above the russet clods the corn is seen
Sprouting its spirey points of tender green
Where squats the hare to terrors wide awake
Like some brown clod the harrows failed to break
While neath the warm hedge boys stray far from home
To crop the early blossoms as they come
Where buttercups will make them eager run
Opening their golden caskets to the sun
To see who shall be first to pluck the prize
And from their hurry up the skylark flies
And oer her half formed nest with happy wings
Winnows the air – till in the clouds she sings
Then hangs a dust spot in the sunny skies
And drops and drops till in her nest she lies
Where boys unheeding past – neer dreaming then

That birds which flew so high – would drop agen
To nests upon the ground where any thing
May come at to destroy had they the wing
Like such a bird themselves would be too proud
And build on nothing but a passing cloud
As free from danger as the heavens are free
From pain and toil – there would they build and be
And sail about the world to scenes unheard
Of and unseen – O where they but a bird
So think they while they listen to its song
And smile and fancy and so pass along
While its low nest moist with the dews of morn
Lye safely with the leveret in the corn

JOHN CLARE

The Sloth

In moving-slow he has no Peer.
You ask him something in his Ear,
He thinks about it for a Year;

And, then, before he says a Word
There, upside down (unlike a Bird),
He will assume that you have Heard –

A most Ex-as-per-at-ing Lug.
But should you call his manner Smug,
He'll sigh and give his Branch a Hug;

Then off again to Sleep he goes,
Still swaying gently by his Toes,
And you just *know* he knows he knows.

THEODORE ROETHKE

The Snail

To grass, or leaf, or fruit, or wall,
The snail sticks close, nor fears to fall,
As if he grew there, house and all
                    Together.

Within that house secure he hides,
When danger imminent betides
Of storm, or other harm besides
                    Of weather.

Give but his horns the slightest touch,
His self-collecting power is such,
He shrinks into his house, with much
                    Displeasure.

Where'er he dwells, he dwells alone,
Except himself has chattels none,
Well satisfied to be his own
                    Whole treasure.

Thus, hermit-like, his life he leads,
Nor partner of his banquet needs,
And if he meets one, only feeds
                    The faster.

Who seeks him must be worse than blind,
(He and his house are so combin'd)
If, finding it, he fails to find
                    Its master.

WILLIAM COWPER

The Snail

   Wise Emblem of our Politick World,
Sage Snail, within thine own self curl'd;
Instruct me softly to make hast,
Whilst these my Feet go slowly fast.

Compendious Snail! thou seem'st to me,
Large *Euclids* strickt Epitome;
And in each Diagram, dost Fling
Thee from the point unto the Ring.
A Figure now Triangulare,
An Oval now, and now a Square;
And then a Serpentine dost crawl
Now a straight Line, now crook'd, now all.
Preventing Rival of the Day,
Th' art up and openest thy Ray,
And ere the Morn cradles the Moon,
Th'art broke into a Beauteous Noon.
Then when the Sun sups in the Deep,
Thy Silver Horns e're *Cinthia*'s peep;
And thou, from thine own liquid Bed
New *Phoebus* heav'st thy pleasant Head.
Who shall a Name for thee create,
Deep Riddle of Mysterious State:
Bold Nature that gives common Birth
To all products of Seas and Earth,
Of thee, as Earth-quakes, is affraid,
Nor will thy dire Deliv'ry aid.
Thou thine own daughter then, and Sire,
That Son and Mother art intire,
That big still with thy self dost go,
And liv'st an aged Embrio;
That like the Cubbs of *India*,
Thou from thy self a while dost play:
But frighted with a Dog or Gun,
In thine own Belly thou dost run,
And as thy House was thine own womb,
So thine own womb, concludes thy tomb.
But now I must (analys'd King)
Thy Oeconomick Virtues sing;
Thou great stay'd Husband still within,
Thou, thee, that's thine dost Discipline;
And when thou art to progress bent,
Thou mov'st thy self and tenement,
As Warlike *Scythians* travayl'd, you
Remove your Men and City too;

Then after a sad Dearth and Rain,
Thou scatterest thy Silver Train;
And when the Trees grow nak'd and old,
Thou cloathest them with Cloth of Gold,
Which from thy Bowels thou dost spin,
And draw from the rich Mines within.
    Now hast thou chang'd thee Saint; and made
Thy self a Fane that's cupula'd;
And in thy wreathed Cloister thou
Walkest thine own Gray fryer too;
Strickt, and lock't up, th'art Hood all ore
And ne'r Eliminat'st thy Dore.
On Sallads thou dost feed severe,
And 'stead of Beads thou drop'st a tear,
And when to rest, each calls the Bell,
Thou sleep'st within thy Marble Cell;
Where in dark contemplation plac'd,
The sweets of Nature thou dost tast;
Who now with Time thy days resolve,
And in a Jelly thee dissolve.
Like a shot Star, which doth repair
Upward, and Rarifie the Air.

RICHARD LOVELACE

Snake

A snake came to my water-trough
On a hot, hot day, and I in pyjamas for the heat,
To drink there.

In the deep, strange-scented shade of the great dark carob-tree
I came down the steps with my pitcher
And must wait, must stand and wait, for there he was at the trough
    before me.

He reached down from a fissure in the earth-wall in the gloom
And trailed his yellow-brown slackness soft-bellied down, over the
    edge of the stone trough

And rested his throat upon the stone bottom,
And where the water had dripped from the tap, in a small clearness,
He sipped with his straight mouth,
Softly drank through his straight gums, into his slack long body,
Silently.

Someone was before me at my water-trough,
And I, like a second comer, waiting.

He lifted his head from his drinking, as cattle do,
And looked at me vaguely, as drinking cattle do,
And flickered his two-forked tongue from his lips, and mused a
    moment,
And stooped and drank a little more,
Being earth-brown, earth-golden from the burning bowels of the earth
On the day of Sicilian July, with Etna smoking.

The voice of my education said to me
He must be killed,
For in Sicily the black, black snakes are innocent, the gold are
    venomous.

And voices in me said, If you were a man
You would take a stick and break him now, and finish him off.

But must I confess how I liked him,
How glad I was he had come like a guest in quiet, to drink at my
    water-trough
And depart peaceful, pacified, and thankless,
Into the burning bowels of this earth?

Was it cowardice, that I dared not kill him?
Was it perversity, that I longed to talk to him?
Was it humility, to feel so honoured?
I felt so honoured.

And yet those voices:
If you were not afraid, you would kill him!

And truly I was afraid, I was most afraid,
But even so, honoured still more
That he should seek my hospitality
From out the dark door of the secret earth.

He drank enough
And lifted his head, dreamily, as one who has drunken,
And flickered his tongue like a forked night on the air, so black,
Seeming to lick his lips,
And looked around like a god, unseeing, into the air,
And slowly turned his head,
And slowly, very slowly, as if thrice adream,
Proceeded to draw his slow length curving round
And climb again the broken bank of my wall-face.

And as he put his head into that dreadful hole,
And as he slowly drew up, snake-easing his shoulders, and entered
    farther,
A sort of horror, a sort of protest against his withdrawing into that
    horrid black hole,
Deliberately going into the blackness, and slowly drawing himself after,
Overcame me now his back was turned.

I looked round, I put down my pitcher,
I picked up a clumsy log
And threw it at the water-trough with a clatter.

I think it did not hit him,
But suddenly that part of him that was left behind convulsed in
  . undignified haste,
Writhed like lightning, and was gone
Into the black hole, the earth-lipped fissure in the wall-front.
At which, in the intense still noon, I stared with fascination.

And immediately I regretted it.
I thought how paltry, how vulgar, what a mean act!
I despised myself and the voices of my accursed human education.

And I thought of the albatross,
And I wished he would come back, my snake.

For he seemed to me again like a king,
Like a king in exile, uncrowned in the underworld,
Now due to be crowned again.

And so, I missed my chance with one of the lords
Of life.
And I have something to expiate;
A pettiness.

D. H. LAWRENCE

The Snare

I hear a sudden cry of pain!
There is a rabbit in a snare:
Now I hear the cry again,
But I cannot tell from where.

But I cannot tell from where
He is calling out for aid!
Crying on the frightened air,
Making everything afraid!

Making everything afraid,
Wrinkling up his little face!
As he cries again for aid;
– And I cannot find the place!

And I cannot find the place
Where his paw is in the snare!
Little One! Oh, Little One!
I am searching everywhere!

JAMES STEPHENS

Snow in the Suburbs

Every branch big with it,
Bent every twig with it;
Every fork like a white web-foot;
Every street and pavement mute:
Some flakes have lost their way, and grope back upward, when

Meeting those meandering down they turn and descend again.
    The palings are glued together like a wall,
    And there is no waft of wind with the fleecy fall.

      A sparrow enters the tree,
      Whereon immediately
    A snow-lump thrice his own slight size
Descends on him and showers his head and eyes,
      And overturns him,
      And near inurns him,
    And lights on a nether twig, when its brush
Starts off a volley of other lodging lumps with a rush.

    The steps are a blanched slope,
    Up which, with feeble hope,
    A black cat comes, wide-eyed and thin;
      And we take him in.

THOMAS HARDY

The Song of the Jellicles

Jellicle Cats come out tonight,
Jellicle Cats come one come all:
The Jellicle Moon is shining bright –
Jellicles come to the Jellicle Ball.

Jellicle Cats are black and white,
Jellicle Cats are rather small;
Jellicle Cats are merry and bright,
And pleasant to hear when they caterwaul.
Jellicle Cats have cheerful faces,
Jellicle Cats have bright black eyes;
They like to practise their airs and graces
And wait for the Jellicle Moon to rise.

    Jellicle Cats develop slowly,
Jellicle Cats are not too big;
Jellicle Cats are roly-poly,
They know how to dance a gavotte and a jig.

Until the Jellicle Moon appears
They make their toilette and take their repose:
Jellicles wash behind their ears,
Jellicles dry between their toes.

  Jellicle Cats are white and black,
Jellicle Cats are of moderate size;
Jellicles jump like a jumping-jack,
Jellicle Cats have moonlit eyes.
They're quiet enough in the morning hours,
They're quiet enough in the afternoon,
Reserving their terpsichorean powers
To dance by the light of the Jellicle Moon.

  Jellicle Cats are black and white,
Jellicle Cats (as I said) are small;
If it happens to be a stormy night
They will practise a caper or two in the hall.
If it happens the sun is shining bright
You would say they had nothing to do at all:
They are resting and saving themselves to be right
For the Jellicle Moon and the Jellicle Ball.

   T. S. ELIOT

from Song of Myself

The butcher-boy puts off his killing-clothes, or sharpens his knife at
    the stall in the market,
I loiter enjoying his repartee and his shuffle and break-down.

Blacksmiths with grimed and hairy chests environ the anvil,
Each has his main-sledge, they are all out, there is a great heat in the
    fire.

From the cinder-strew'd threshold I follow their movements,
The lithe sheer of their waists plays even with their massive arms,
Overhand the hammers swing, overhand so slow, overhand so sure,
They do not hasten, each man hits in his place.

The negro holds firmly the reins of his four horses, the block swags
    underneath on its tied-over chain,
The negro that drives the long dray of the stone-yard, steady and tall
    he stands pois'd on one leg on the string-piece,
His blue shirt exposes his ample neck and breast and loosens over his
    hip-band,
His glance is calm and commanding, he tosses the slouch of his hat
    away from his forehead,
The sun falls on his crispy hair and mustache, falls on the black of his
    polish'd and perfect limbs.

I behold the picturesque giant and love him, and I do not stop there,
I go with the team also.

In me the caresser of life wherever moving, backward as well as forward
    sluing
To niches aside and junior bending, not a person or object missing,
Absorbing all to myself and for this song.

Oxen that rattle the yoke and chain or halt in the leafy shade, what is
    that you express in your eyes?
It seems to me more than all the print I have read in my life.

My tread scares the wood-drake and wood-duck on my distant and
    day-long ramble,
They rise together, they slowly circle around.

I believe in those wing'd purposes,
And acknowledge red, yellow, white, playing within me,
And consider green and violet and the tufted crown intentional,
And do not call the tortoise unworthy because she is not something
    else,
And the jay in the woods never studied the gamut, yet trills pretty well
    to me,
And the look of the bay mare shames silliness out of me.

The wild gander leads his flock through the cool night,
Ya-honk he says, and sounds it down to me like an invitation,
The pert may suppose it meaningless, but I listening close,
Find its purpose and place up there toward the wintry sky.

The sharp-hoof'd moose of the north, the cat on the house-sill, the
    chickadee, the prairie-dog,

The litter of the grunting sow as they tug at her teats,
The brood of the turkey-hen and she with her half-spread wings,
I see in them and myself the same old law.

The press of my foot to the earth springs a hundred affections,
They scorn the best I can do to relate them.

I am enamour'd of growing out-doors,
Of men that live among cattle or taste of the ocean or woods,
Of the builders and steerers of ships and the wielders of axes and
    mauls, and the drivers of horses,
I can eat and sleep with them week in and week out.

What is commonest, cheapest, nearest, easiest, is Me,
Me going in for my chances, spending for vast returns,
Adorning myself to bestow myself on the first that will take me,
Not asking the sky to come down to my good will,
Scattering it freely forever.

I think I could turn and live awhile with the animals . . . they are so
    placid and self-contained,
I stand and look at them sometimes half the day long.
They do not sweat and whine about their condition,
They do not lie awake in the dark and weep for their sins,
They do not make me sick discussing their duty to God,
Not one is dissatisfied . . . not one is demented with the mania of
    owning things,
Not one kneels to another nor to his kind that lived thousands of years
    ago,
Not one is respectable or industrious over the whole earth.

So they show their relations to me and I accept them;
They bring me tokens of myself . . . they evince them plainly in their
    possession.

I do not know where they got those tokens,
I must have passed that way untold times ago and negligently dropt
    them,
Myself moving forward then and now and forever,
Gathering and showing more always and with velocity,

Infinite and omnigenous and the like of these among them;
Not too exclusive toward the reachers of my remembrancers,
Picking out here one that shall be my amie,
Choosing to go with him on brotherly terms.

A gigantic beauty of a stallion, fresh and responsive to my caresses,
Head high in the forehead and wide between the ears,
Limbs glossy and supple, tail dusting the ground,
Eyes well apart and full of sparkling wickedness . . . ears finely cut and
    flexibly moving.

His nostrils dilate . . . my heels embrace him . . . his well built limbs
    tremble with pleasure . . . we speed around and return.

I but use you a moment and then I resign you stallion . . . and do not
    need your paces, and outgallop them,
And myself as I stand or sit pass faster than you.

Swift wind! Space! My Soul! Now I know it is true what I guessed at;
What I guessed when I loafed on the grass,
What I guessed while I lay alone in my bed . . . and again as I walked
    the beach under the paling stars of the morning.

My ties and ballasts leave me . . . I travel . . . I sail . . . my elbows rest
    in the sea-gaps,
I skirt the sierras . . . my palms cover continents,
I am afoot with my vision.

By the city's quadrangular houses . . . in log-huts, or camping with
    lumbermen,
Along the ruts of the turnpike . . . along the dry gulch and rivulet bed,
Hoeing my onion-patch, and rows of carrots and parsnips . . . crossing
    savannas . . . trailing in forests,
Prospecting . . . gold-digging . . . girdling the trees of a new purchase,
Scorched ankle-deep by the hot sand . . . hauling my boat down the
    shallow river;
Where the panther walks to and fro on a limb overhead . . . where the
    buck turns furiously at the hunter,
Where the rattlesnake suns his flabby length on a rock . . . where the
    otter is feeding on fish,
Where the alligator in his tough pimples sleeps by the bayou,
Where the black bear is searching for roots or honey . . . where the
    beaver pats the mud with his paddle-tail;

Over the growing sugar . . . over the cottonplant . . . over the rice in
    its low moist field;
Over the sharp-peaked farmhouse with its scalloped scum and slender
    shoots from the gutters;
Over the western persimmon . . . over the longleaved corn and the
    delicate blue-flowered flax;
Over the white and brown buckwheat, a hummer and a buzzer there
    with the rest,
Over the dusky green of the rye as it ripples and shades in the breeze;
Scaling mountains . . . pulling myself cautiously up . . . holding on by
    low scragged limbs,
Walking the path worn in the grass and beat through the leaves of the
    brush;
Where the quail is whistling betwixt the woods and the wheatlot,
Where the bat flies in the July eve . . . where the great goldbug drops
    through the dark;
Where the flails keep time on the barn floor,
Where the brook puts out of the roots of the old tree and flows to the
    meadow,
Where cattle stand and shake away flies with the tremulous shuddering
    of their hides,
Where the cheese-cloth hangs in the kitchen, and andirons straddle the
    hearth-slab, and cobwebs fall in festoons from the rafters;
Where triphammers crash . . . where the press is whirling its cylinders;
Wherever the human heart beats with terrible throes out of its ribs;
Where the pear-shaped balloon is floating aloft . . . floating in it myself
    and looking composedly down;
Where the life-car is drawn on the slipnose . . . where the heat hatches
    pale-green eggs in the dented sand,
Where the she-whale swims with her calves and never forsakes them,
Where the steamship trails hindways its long pennant of smoke,
Where the ground-shark's fin cuts like a black chip out of the water,
Where the half-burned brig is riding on unknown currents,
Where shells grow to her slimy deck, and the dead are corrupting
    below;
Where the striped and starred flag is borne at the head of the regiments;
Approaching Manhattan, up by the long-stretching island,
Under Niagara, the cataract falling like a veil over my countenance;
Upon a door-step . . . upon the horse-block of hard wood outside,

Upon the race-course, or enjoying pic-nics or jigs or a good game of
base-ball,
At he-festivals with blackguard jibes and ironical license and bull-
dances and drinking and laughter,
At the cider-mill, tasting the sweet of the brown squash . . . sucking
the juice through a straw,
At apple-pealings, wanting kisses for all the red fruit I find,
At musters and beach-parties and friendly bees and huskings and house-
raisings;
Where the mockingbird sounds his delicious gurgles, and cackles and
screams and weeps,
Where the hay-rick stands in the barnyard, and the dry-stalks are
scattered, and the brood cow waits in the hovel,
Where the bull advances to do his masculine work, and the stud to the
mare, and the cock is treading the hen,
Where the heifers browse, and the geese nip their food with short jerks;
Where the sundown shadows lengthen over the limitless and lonesome
prairie,
Where the herds of buffalo make a crawling spread of the square miles
far and near;
Where the hummingbird shimmers . . . where the neck of the longlived
swan is curving and winding;
Where the laughing-gull scoots by the slappy shore and laughs her
near-human laugh;
Where beehives range on a gray bench in the garden half-hid by the
high weeds;
Where the band-necked partridges roost in a ring on the ground with
their heads out;
Where burial coaches enter the arched gates of a cemetery;
Where winter wolves bark amid wastes of snow and icicled trees;
Where the yellow-crowned heron comes to the edge of the marsh at
night and feeds upon small crabs;
Where the splash of swimmers and divers cools the warm noon;
Where the katydid works her chromatic reed on the walnut-tree over
the well;

WALT WHITMAN

The Swarm

Somebody is shooting at something in our town –
A dull pom, pom in the Sunday street.
Jealousy can open the blood,
It can make black roses.
Who are they shooting at?

It is you the knives are out for
At Waterloo, Waterloo, Napoleon,
The hump of Elba on your short back,
And the snow, marshaling its brilliant cutlery
Mass after mass, saying Shh!

Shh! These are chess people you play with,
Still figures of ivory.
The mud squirms with throats,
Stepping stones for French bootsoles.
The gilt and pink domes of Russia melt and float off

In the furnace of greed. Clouds, clouds.
So the swarm balls and deserts
Seventy feet up, in a black pine tree.
It must be shot down. Pom! Pom!
So dumb it thinks bullets are thunder.

It thinks they are the voice of God
Condoning the beak, the claw, the grin of the dog
Yellow-haunched, a pack-dog,
Grinning over its bone of ivory
Like the pack, the pack, like everybody.

The bees have got so far. Seventy feet high!
Russia, Poland and Germany!
The mild hills, the same old magenta
Fields shrunk to a penny
Spun into a river, the river crossed.

The bees argue, in their black ball,
A flying hedgehog, all prickles.
The man with gray hands stands under the honeycomb
Of their dream, the hived station
Where trains, faithful to their steel arcs,

Leave and arrive, and there is no end to the country.
Pom! Pom! They fall
Dismembered, to a tod of ivy.
So much for the charioteers, the outriders, the Grand Army!
A red tatter, Napoleon!

The last badge of victory.
The swarm is knocked into a cocked straw hat.
Elba, Elba, bleb on the sea!
The white busts of marshals, admirals, generals
Worming themselves into niches.

How instructive this is!
The dumb, banded bodies
Walking the plank draped with Mother France's upholstery
Into a new mausoleum,
An ivory palace, a crotch pine.

The man with gray hands smiles –
The smile of a man of business, intensely practical.
They are not hands at all
But asbestos receptacles.
Pom! Pom! 'They would have killed *me*.'

Stings big as drawing pins!
It seems bees have a notion of honor,
A black intractable mind.
Napoleon is pleased, he is pleased with everything.
O Europe! O ton of honey!

SYLVIA PLATH

Sweet Road

As though the light
were salving your wounds . . .

and the bees flying very low . . .

and the camber sweet
with their crushed black-and-amber.

MARIN SORESCU
Translated from the Romanian by Paul Muldoon with Joana Russell-Gebbett

Take One Home for the Kiddies

On shallow straw, in shadeless glass,
Huddled by empty bowls, they sleep:
No dark, no dam, no earth, no grass –
Mam, get us one of them to keep.

Living toys are something novel,
But it soon wears off somehow.
Fetch the shoebox, fetch the shovel –
Mam, we're playing funerals now.

PHILIP LARKIN

Tamer and Hawk

I thought I was so tough,
But gentled at your hands,
Cannot be quick enough
To fly for you and show
That when I go I go
At your commands.

Even in flight above
I am no longer free:

You seeled me with your love,
I am blind to other birds –
The habit of your words
Has hooded me.

As formerly, I wheel
I hover and I twist,
But only want the feel,
In my possessive thought,
Of catcher and of caught
Upon your wrist.

You but half civilize,
Taming me in this way.
Through having only eyes
For you I fear to lose,
I lose to keep, and choose
Tamer as prey.

THOM GUNN

Thirteen Ways of Looking at a Blackbird

I

Among twenty snowy mountains,
The only moving thing
Was the eye of the blackbird.

II

I was of three minds,
Like a tree
In which there are three blackbirds.

III

The blackbird whirled in the autumn winds.
It was a small part of the pantomime.

IV

A man and a woman
Are one.
A man and a woman and a blackbird
Are one.

V

I do not know which to prefer,
The beauty of inflections
Or the beauty of innuendoes,
The blackbird whistling
Or just after.

VI

Icicles filled the long window
With barbaric glass.
The shadow of the blackbird
Crossed it, to and fro.
The mood
Traced in the shadow
An indecipherable cause.

VII

O thin men of Haddam,
Why do you imagine golden birds?
Do you not see how the blackbird
Walks around the feet
Of the women about you?

VIII

I know noble accents
And lucid, inescapable rhythms;
But I know, too,
That the blackbird is involved
In what I know.

IX

When the blackbird flew out of sight,
It marked the edge
Of one of many circles.

X

At the sight of blackbirds
Flying in a green light,
Even the bawds of euphony
Would cry out sharply.

XI

He rode over Connecticut
In a glass coach.
Once, a fear pierced him,
In that he mistook
The shadow of his equipage
For blackbirds.

XII

The river is moving.
The blackbird must be flying.

XIII

It was evening all afternoon.
It was snowing
And it was going to snow.
The blackbird sat
In the cedar-limbs.

WALLACE STEVENS

This Little Pig

This little pig went to market;
This little pig stayed at home;
This little pig had roast beef;
This little pig had none;
And this little pig cried, Wee-wee-wee!
  All the way home.

ANONYMOUS

The Thought-Fox

I imagine this midnight moment's forest:
Something else is alive
Beside the clock's loneliness
And this blank page where my fingers move.

Through the window I see no star:
Something more near
Though deeper within darkness
Is entering the loneliness:

Cold, delicately as the dark snow,
A fox's nose touches twig, leaf;
Two eyes serve a movement, that now
And again now, and now, and now

Sets neat prints into the snow
Between trees, and warily a lame
Shadow lags by stump and in hollow
Of a body that is bold to come

Across clearings, an eye,
A widening deepening greenness,
Brilliantly, concentratedly,
Coming about its own business

Till, with a sudden sharp hot stink of fox
It enters the dark hole of the head.
The window is starless still; the clock ticks,
The page is printed.

TED HUGHES

t,h;r:u;s,h;e:s

are
silent
now

.in silverly

notqu
-it-
eness

dre(is)ams

a
the
o

f moon

E. E. CUMMINGS

Thrushes

Terrifying are the attent sleek thrushes on the lawn,
More coiled steel than living – a poised
Dark deadly eye, those delicate legs
Triggered to stirrings beyond sense – with a start, a bounce, a stab
Overtake the instant and drag out some writhing thing.
No indolent procrastinations and no yawning stares,
No sighs or head-scratchings. Nothing but bounce and stab
And a ravening second.

Is it their single-mind-sized skulls, or a trained
Body, or genius, or a nestful of brats
Gives their days this bullet and automatic
Purpose? Mozart's brain had it, and the shark's mouth
That hungers down the blood-smell even to a leak of its own
Side and devouring of itself: efficiency which
Strikes too streamlined for any doubt to pluck at it
Or obstruction deflect.

With a man it is otherwise. Heroisms on horseback,
Outstripping his desk-diary at a broad desk,
Carving at a tiny ivory ornament
For years: his act worships itself – while for him,
Though he bends to be blent in the prayer, how loud and above what

Furious spaces of fire do the distracting devils
Orgy and hosannah, under what wilderness
Of black silent waters weep.

TED HUGHES

To a Butterfly

Stay near me – do not take thy flight!
A little longer stay in sight!
Much converse do I find in thee,
Historian of my infancy!
Float near me; do not yet depart!
Dead times revive in thee:
Thou bring'st, gay creature as thou art!
A solemn image to my heart,
My father's family!

Oh! pleasant, pleasant were the days,
The time, when in our childish plays,
My sister Emmeline and I
Together chased the butterfly!
A very hunter did I rush
Upon the prey; – with leaps and springs
I followed on from brake to bush;
But she, God love her! feared to brush
The dust from off its wings.

WILLIAM WORDSWORTH

To the Cuckoo

O blithe New-comer! I have heard,
I hear thee and rejoice.
O Cuckoo! shall I call thee Bird,
Or but a wandering Voice?

While I am lying on the grass
Thy twofold shout I hear;
From hill to hill it seems to pass
At once far off, and near.

Though babbling only to the Vale,
Of sunshine and of flowers,
Thou bringest unto me a tale
Of visionary hours.

Thrice welcome, darling of the Spring!
Even yet thou art to me
No bird, but an invisible thing,
A voice, a mystery;

The same whom in my schoolboy days
I listened to; that Cry
Which made me look a thousand ways
In bush, and tree, and sky.

To seek thee did I often rove
Through woods and on the green;
And thou wert still a hope, a love;
Still longed for, never seen.

And I can listen to thee yet;
Can lie upon the plain
And listen, till I do beget
That golden time again.

O blessed Bird! the earth we pace
Again appears to be
An unsubstantial, faery place;
That is fit home for Thee!

WILLIAM WORDSWORTH

To the Ladybug

Ladybug, ladybug,
  Fly away home,

Your house is on fire
  Your children all gone;
All but one,
  And her name is Ann,
And she has crept under
  The warming pan.

ANONYMOUS

To a Louse, On Seeing one on a Lady's Bonnet at Church

Ha! whare ye gaun, ye crowlan ferlie!
Your impudence protects you sairly:
I canna say but ye strunt rarely,
    Owre *gawze* and *lace*;
Tho' faith, I fear ye dine but sparely,
    On sic a place.

Ye ugly, creepan, blastet wonner,
Detested, shunn'd, by saunt an' sinner,
How daur ye set your fit upon her,
    Sae fine a *Lady*!
Gae somewhere else and seek your dinner,
    On some poor body.

Swith, in some beggar's haffet squattle;
There ye may creep, and sprawl, and sprattle,
Wi' ither kindred, jumping cattle,
    In shoals and nations;
Whare *horn* nor *bane* ne'er daur unsettle,
    Your thick plantations.

Now haud you there, ye're out o' sight,
Below the fatt'rels, snug and tight,
Na faith ye yet! ye'll no be right,
    Till ye've got on it,
The vera tapmost, towrin height
    O' *Miss's bonnet*.

My sooth! right bauld ye set your nose out,
As plump an' gray as onie grozet:
O for some rank, mercurial rozet,
        Or fell, red smeddum,
I'd gie you sic a hearty dose o't,
        Wad dress your droddum!

I wad na been surpriz'd to spy
You on an auld wife's *flainen toy*;
Or aiblins some bit duddie boy,
        On 's *wylecoat*;
But Miss's fine *Lunardi*, fye!
  How daur ye do 't?

O *Jenny* dinna toss your head,
An' set your beauties a' abread!
Ye little ken what cursed speed
        The blastie 's makin!
Thae *winks* and *finger-ends*, I dread,
        Are notice takin!

O wad some Pow'r the giftie gie us
To see oursels as others see us!
It wad frae monie a blunder free us
        An' foolish notion:
What airs in dress an' gait wad lea'e us,
        And ev'n Devotion!

ROBERT BURNS

To a Mouse, On Turning her up in her Nest, with the Plough, November, 1785

Wee, sleeket, cowran, tim'ous *beastie*,
O, what a panic's in my breastie!
Thou need na start awa sae hasty,
        Wi' bickering brattle!
I wad be laith to rin an' chase thee,
        Wi' murd'ring *pattle*!

I'm truly sorry Man's dominion
Has broken Nature's social union,
An' justifies that ill opinion,
    Which makes thee startle,
At me, thy poor, earth-born companion,
    An' *fellow-mortal*!

I doubt na, whyles, but thou may *thieve*;
What then? poor beastie, thou maun live!
A *daimen-icker* in a *thrave*
    'S a sma' request:
I'll get a blessin wi' the lave,
    An' never miss't!

Thy wee-bit *housie*, too, in ruin!
It's silly wa's the win's are strewin!
An' naething, now, to big a new ane,
    O' foggage green!
An' bleak *December's winds* ensuin,
    Baith snell an' keen!

Thou saw the fields laid bare an' wast,
An' weary *Winter* comin fast,
An' cozie here, beneath the blast,
    Thou thought to dwell,
Till crash! the cruel *coulter* past
    Out thro' thy cell.

That wee-bit heap o' leaves an' stibble,
Has cost thee monie a weary nibble!
Now thou 's turn'd out, for a' thy trouble,
    But house or hald,
To thole the Winter's *sleety dribble*,
    An' *cranreuch* cauld!

But Mousie, thou art no thy-lane,
In proving *foresight* may be vain:
The best laid schemes o' *Mice* an' *Men*,
    Gang aft agley,
An' lea'e us nought but grief an' pain,
    For promis'd joy!

Still, thou art blest, compar'd wi' *me*!

The *present* only toucheth thee:
But Och! I *backward* cast my e'e,
    On prospects drear!
An' *forward*, tho' I canna *see*,
    I *guess* an' *fear*!

ROBERT BURNS

To a Sky-Lark

Hail to thee, blithe Spirit!
  Bird thou never wert –
That from Heaven, or near it,
  Pourest thy full heart
In profuse strains of unpremeditated art.

Higher still and higher
  From the earth thou springest
Like a cloud of fire;
  The blue deep thou wingest,
And singing still dost soar, and soaring ever singest.

In the golden lightning
  Of the sunken Sun –
O'er which clouds are brightning,
  Thou dost float and run;
Like an unbodied joy whose race is just begun.

The pale purple even
  Melts around thy flight,
Like a star of Heaven
  In the broad day-light
Thou art unseen, – but yet I hear thy shrill delight,

Keen as are the arrows
  Of that silver sphere,
Whose intense lamp narrows
  In the white dawn clear
Until we hardly see – we feel that it is there.

All the earth and air
  With thy voice is loud,
As when Night is bare
  From one lonely cloud
The moon rains out her beams – and Heaven is overflowed.

What thou art we know not;
  What is most like thee?
From rainbow clouds there flow not
  Drops so bright to see
As from thy presence showers a rain of melody.

Like a Poet hidden
  In the light of thought,
Singing hymns unbidden,
  Till the world is wrought
To sympathy with hopes and fears it heeded not:

Like a high-born maiden
  In a palace-tower,
Soothing her love-laden
  Soul in secret hour,
With music sweet as love – which overflows her bower:

Like a glow-worm golden
  In a dell of dew,
Scattering unbeholden
  Its aerial hue
Among the flowers and grass which screen it from the view:

Like a rose embowered
  In its own green leaves –
By warm winds deflowered –
  Till the scent it gives
Makes faint with too much sweet these heavy-winged thieves:

Sound of vernal showers
  On the twinkling grass,
Rain-awakened flowers,
  All that ever was
Joyous, and clear and fresh, thy music doth surpass.

Teach us, Sprite or Bird,

What sweet thoughts are thine;
　I have never heard
　　Praise of love or wine
That panted forth a flood of rapture so divine:

　Chorus Hymeneal
　　Or triumphal chaunt
　Matched with thine would be all
　　But an empty vaunt,
A thing wherein we feel there is some hidden want.

　What objects are the fountains
　　Of thy happy strain?
　What fields or waves or mountains?
　　What shapes of sky or plain?
What love of thine own kind? what ignorance of pain?

　With thy clear keen joyance
　　Languor cannot be –
　Shadow of annoyance
　　Never came near thee;
Thou lovest – but ne'er knew love's sad satiety.

　Waking or asleep,
　　Thou of death must deem
　Things more true and deep
　　Than we mortals dream,
Or how could thy notes flow in such a chrystal stream?

　We look before and after,
　　And pine for what is not –
　Our sincerest laughter
　　With some pain is fraught –
Our sweetest songs are those that tell of saddest thought.

　Yet if we could scorn
　　Hate and pride and fear;
　If we were things born
　　Not to shed a tear,
I know not how thy joy we ever should come near.

　Better than all measures
　　Of delightful sound –

Better than all treasures
    That in books are found –
Thy skill to poet were, thou Scorner of the ground!

Teach me half the gladness
    That thy brain must know,
Such harmonious madness
    From my lips would flow
The world should listen then – as I am listening now.

PERCY BYSSHE SHELLEY

To a Skylark

Ethereal minstrel! pilgrim of the sky!
Dost thou despise the earth where cares abound?
Or, while the wings aspire, are heart and eye
Both with thy nest upon the dewy ground?
Thy nest which thou canst drop into at will,
Those quivering wings composed, that music still!

Leave to the nightingale her shady wood;
A privacy of glorious light is thine;
Whence thou dost pour upon the world a flood
Of harmony, with instinct more divine;
Type of the wise who soar, but never roam;
True to the kindred points of Heaven and Home!

WILLIAM WORDSWORTH

To a Snail

If 'compression is the first grace of style,'
you have it. Contractility is a virtue
as modesty is a virtue.
It is not the acquisition of any one thing
that is able to adorn,

or the incidental quality that occurs
as a concomitant of something well said,
that we value in style,
but the principle that is hid:
in the absence of feet, 'a method of conclusions';
'a knowledge of principles,'
in the curious phenomenon of your occipital horn.

MARIANNE MOORE

To a Squirrel at Kyle-na-no

Come play with me;
Why should you run
Through the shaking tree
As though I'd a gun
To strike you dead?
When all I would do
Is to scratch your head
And let you go.

W. B. YEATS

To a Young Ass

Its Mother being tethered near it

Poor little Foal of an oppressed Race!
I love the languid Patience of thy face:
And oft with gentle hand I give thee bread,
And clap thy ragged Coat, and pat thy head.
But what thy dulled Spirits hath dismayed,
That never thou dost sport along the glade?
And (most unlike the nature of things young)
That earthward still thy moveless head is hung?
Do thy prophetic Fears anticipate,
Meek Child of Misery! thy future fate?

The starving meal, and all the thousand aches
'Which patient Merit of the Unworthy takes'?
Or is thy sad heart thrilled with filial pain
To see thy wretched Mother's shorten'd Chain?
And truly, very piteous is her Lot –
Chained to a Log within a narrow spot,
Where the close-eaten Grass is scarcely seen,
While sweet around her waves the tempting Green!
Poor Ass! thy master should have learnt to show
Pity – best taught by fellowship of Woe!
For much I fear me that He lives like thee,
Half famished in a land of Luxury!
How askingly its footsteps hither bend,
It seems to say, 'And have I then one Friend?'
Innocent Foal! thou poor despised Forlorn!
I hail thee Brother – spite of the fool's scorn!
And fain would take thee with me, in the Dell
Of Peace and mild Equality to dwell,
Where Toil shall call the charmer Health his bride,
And Laughter tickle Plenty's ribless side!
How thou wouldst toss thy heels in gamesome play,
And frisk about, as lamb or kitten gay!
Yea! and more musically sweet to me
Thy dissonant harsh bray of joy would be,
Than warbled melodies that soothe to rest
The aching of pale Fashion's vacant breast!

SAMUEL TAYLOR COLERIDGE

To the Snipe

Lover of swamps
The quagmire overgrown
With hassock tufts of sedge – where fear encamps
Around thy home alone

The trembling grass
Quakes from the human foot
Nor bears the weight of man to let him pass
Where he alone and mute

Sitteth at rest
In safety neath the clump
Of hugh flag-forrest that thy haunts invest
Or some old sallow stump

Thriving on seams
That tiney islands swell
Just hilling from the mud and rancid streams
Suiting thy nature well

For here thy bill
Suited by wisdom good
Of rude unseemly length doth delve and drill
The gelid mass for food

And here may hap
When summer suns hath drest
The moors rude desolate and spungy lap
May hide thy mystic nest

Mystic indeed
For isles that ocean make
Are scarcely more secure for birds to build
Then this flag-hidden lake

Boys thread the woods
To their remotest shades
But in these marshy flats these stagnant floods
Security pervades

From year to year
Places untrodden lye
Where man nor boy nor stock hath ventured near
– Nought gazed on but the sky

And fowl that dread
The very breath of man
Hiding in spots that never knew his tread
A wild and timid clan

Wigeon and teal
And wild duck – restless lot
That from mans dreaded sight will ever steal
To the most dreary spot

Here tempests howl
Around each flaggy plot
Where they who dread mans sight the water fowl
Hide and are frighted not

Tis power divine
That heartens them to brave
The roughest tempest and at ease recline
On marshes or the wave

Yet instinct knows
Not safetys bounds to shun
The firmer ground where skulking fowler goes
With searching dogs and gun

By tepid springs
Scarcely one stride across
Though brambles from its edge a shelter flings
Thy safety is at loss

And never chuse
The little sinky foss
Streaking the moores whence spa-red water spews
From puddles fringed with moss

Free booters there
Intent to kill and slay
Startle with cracking guns the trepid air
And dogs thy haunts betray

From dangers reach
Here thou art safe to roam
Far as these washy flag-worn marshes stretch
A still and quiet home

In these thy haunts
Ive gleaned habitual love
From the vague world where pride and folly taunts
I muse and look above

Thy solitudes
The unbounded heaven esteems
And here my heart warms into higher moods
And dignifying dreams

I see the sky
Smile on the meanest spot
Giving to all that creep or walk or flye
A calm and cordial lot

Thine teaches me
Right feelings to employ
That in the dreariest places peace will be
A dweller and a joy

JOHN CLARE

Toad

Stop looking like a purse. How could a purse
squeeze under the rickety door and sit,
full of satisfaction, in a man's house?

You clamber towards me on your four corners –
right hand, left foot, left hand, right foot.

I love you for being a toad,
for crawling like a Japanese wrestler,
and for not being frightened.

I put you in my purse hand, not shutting it,
and set you down outside directly under
every star.

A jewel in your head? Toad,
you've put one in mine,
a tiny radiance in a dark place.

NORMAN MACCAIG

The Trout

For Barrie Cooke

Flat on the bank I parted
Rushes to ease my hands
In the water without a ripple
And tilt them slowly downstream
To where he lay, tendril-light,
In his fluid sensual dream.

Bodiless lord of creation,
I hung briefly above him
Savouring my own absence,
Senses expanding in the slow
Motion, the photographic calm
That grows before action.

As the curve of my hands
Swung under his body
He surged, with visible pleasure.
I was so preternaturally close
I could count every stipple
But still cast no shadow, until

The two palms crossed in a cage
Under the lightly pulsing gills.
Then (entering my own enlarged
Shape, which rode on the water)
I gripped. To this day I can
Taste his terror on my hands.

JOHN MONTAGUE

Turkeys

The turkeys wade the close to catch the bees
In the old border full of maple trees
And often lay away and breed and come
And bring a brood of chelping chickens home

The turkey gobbles loud and drops his rag
And struts and sprunts his tail and drags
His wing on ground and makes a huzzing noise
Nauntles at passer bye and drives the boys
And bounces up and flyes at passer bye
The old dogs snaps and grins nor ventures nigh
He gobbles loud and drives the boys from play
They throw their sticks and kick away
And turn agen the stone comes huzzing bye
He drops his quiet tail and forced to flye

Draws up his scarlet snout and cools to grey
And drops his gobble noise and sneaks away
He drives the noisey ducks as soon as loose
And fights with awkard haste the hissing goose
And tramples round and fairly beats him down
And quarrels with the maidens sunday gown
He often gives the cock and hens the chase
And drives the stranger till he leaves the place
And runs and gobbles up and when he beats
They all come up and follow the retreat
And when a beggar comes he nauntling steals
And gobbles loud and pecks the strangers heels
He fights the dunghill cock that quarrels hard
And hobbles round the master of the yard

The idle turkey gobbling half the day
Goes hobbling through the grass and lays away
Five and red spotted eggs where many pass
But none ere thinks of turkeys in the grass
The old dogs sees her on and goes away
The old dame calls and wonders where they lay
Among the old and thickest grass they lie
The fox unnotices and passes bye
The blackbird breeds above a cunning guest
And hides the shells cause none should find the nest
The old crow crawks around them every day

And trys to steal the turkeys eggs away
The magpie cackles round for any prey
And finds the wounded snake and goes away

JOHN CLARE

The Twa Corbies

As I was walking all alane,
I heard twa corbies making a mane;
The tane unto the t'other say,
'Where sall we gang and dine to-day?'

'In behint you auld fail dike,
I wot there lies a new slain knight;
And naebody kens that he lies there,
But his hawk, his hound, and lady fair.

'His hound is to the hunting gane,
His hawk to fetch the wild-fowl hame,
His lady's ta'en another mate,
So we may mak our dinner sweet.

'Ye'll sit on his white hause-bane,
And I'll pike out his bonny blue een;
Wi' ae lock o' his gowden hair
We'll theek our nest when it grows bare.

'Mony a one for him makes mane,
But nane sall ken where he is gane;
O'er his white banes, when they are bare,
The wind sall blaw for evermair.'

ANONYMOUS

Two Dogs

Enchantment creek underbank pollen, are the stiff scents he makes,
hot grass rolling and rabbit-dig but only saliva chickweed.
Road pizza clay bird, hers answer him, rot-spiced good. Blady grass,
she adds, ant log in hot sunshine. Snake two sunups back. Orifice?
Orifice, he wriggles. Night fox? Night fox, with left pad wound.
Cement bag, hints his shoulder. Catmeat, boasts his tail, twice enjoyed.
Folded sapless inside me, she clenches. He retracts initial blood.
Frosty darks coming, he nuzzles. High wind rock human-free howl,
her different law. Soon. Away, away, eucalypts speeding –
Bark! I water for it. Her eyes go binocular, as in pawed
hop frog snack play. Come ploughed, she jumps, ground. Bark tractor,
white bitterhead grub and pull scarecrow. Me! assents his urine.

LES MURRAY

Two Dogs on a Pub Roof

There are two dogs on a pub roof.
One's called Garth, the other Rolf.
Both are loud – but don't think they're all mouth.
I've been watching them and it's my belief
that they've been posted there, not quite on earth,
as emissaries of some higher truth
it's our job to get to the bottom of,
if only we can sort out the pith from the guff.
Garth's bark's no ordinary *woof, woof*:
it's a full-throttle affair, like whooping-cough,
a racking hack that shakes him from scruff
to tail in hour-long binges of holding forth
on all manner of obsessive stuff,
from pigeons and planes to not getting enough
to eat and so being ready to bite your head off.
He's whipped up in a perpetual froth
of indignation on his own behalf.
Poof! Dwarf! Oaf! Filth!
These and suchlike are among his chief

forms of salutation – and he means you, guv!
His whole philosophy, his pennyworth,
is 'All's enemy that's not self'
(with the provisional exception of his brother Rolf).
It's no joke and you don't feel inclined to laugh.
Rolf's even more frightening: his *arf! arf!*
seems designed to tear the sky in half,
every utterance an ultimate expletive,
every one a barbed shaft
aimed accurately at your midriff
and transfixing you with impotent wrath.
You and him. It bothers you both.
The thing's reciprocal, a north-south
axis that skewers the two of you like love.
You're David and Goliath, Peter and the Wolf,
Robin Hood and his Sheriff, Mutt and Jeff –
any ding-donging duo from history or myth
that's come to stand as a hieroglyph
for eternal foedom, non-stop strife,
the old Manichean fisticuffs
without which there'd be no story, no life,
and the whole cycle of birth, breath,
scoff, boff, graft, grief and death
would amount to so much waste of puff.
You're spiritual partners, hand in glove,
you and Rolfie, you and Garth,
you and the two of them up on that roof,
barking and hopping, acting tough,
flinging their taunts across the gulf
of the entire neighbourhood: *You lot down beneath!*
You got a diabolical nerve!
Who gave you permission to breathe?
This is our gaff! This is our turf!
Don't even think of crossing our path,
if you happen to value what remains of your health!
One false move and we'll show you teeth . . .
And so on. Of course, that's only a rough
translation, but it will more or less serve,
being at least the gist of the riff
that bores you mad and drives you stiff

all day long. Night, too. Nights, they work shifts.
One sleeps, while the other faces the brave
task of keeping the moon at a safe
distance and making sure the stars behave.
Which is why there are two of them. If
you've begun to wonder. As you no doubt have.
Then sometimes they'll mount an all-night rave,
Garth dancing with Rolf, Rolf with Garth –
though there's nothing queer about these two psychopaths –
and you're the inevitable wallflower, on the shelf,
surplus to requirements. Only you can't stay aloof.
Like it or lump it, you're stuck in their groove.
The joint's jumping in every joist and lath
and nobody, but nobody, is going to leave.
You're as free an agent as the flame-fazed moth
that's in thrall, flamboyantly befuddled, and not fireproof.
You're party to the party, however loth.
You belong along. You're kin. You're kith.
You're living testimony to the preposition 'with'.
You're baby, bathwater and bath.
So don't dash out with your Kalashnikov
and hope to cut a definitive swathe
through the opposition. Don't throw that Molotov
cocktail. Put down that Swiss Army knife.
Stop spitting. Stop sputtering. Don't fluster. Don't faff.
And don't be so daft, naff, duff or uncouth
as to think you're calling anyone's bluff –
let alone that of the powers above –
by threatening to depart in a huff.
They are your world, where you live,
and this is what their telegraph
of yaps and yelps, their salvoes of snuff-
sneezes, their one-note arias, oath-
fests and dog-demagoguery, their throes of gruff
throat-flexing and guffaws without mirth
are meant to signify. And it's all for your behoof!
So thanks be to Garth, and thanks to Rolf –
those two soothsayers with their one sooth,

pontificating on that pub roof –
and thanks to the God who created them both
for your enlightenment and as proof of His ruth!

CHRISTOPHER REID

The Tyger

Tyger Tyger, burning bright,
In the forests of the night;
What immortal hand or eye,
Could frame thy fearful symmetry?

In what distant deeps or skies
Burnt the fire of thine eyes?
On what wings dare he aspire?
What the hand, dare sieze the fire?

And what shoulder, & what art,
Could twist the sinews of thy heart?
And when thy heart began to beat,
What dread hand? & what dread feet?

What the hammer? what the chain,
In what furnace was thy brain?
What the anvil? what dread grasp,
Dare its deadly terrors clasp!

When the stars threw down their spears
And water'd heaven with their tears:
Did he smile his work to see?
Did he who made the Lamb make thee?

Tyger Tyger burning bright,
In the forests of the night:
What immortal hand or eye,
Dare frame thy fearful symmetry?

WILLIAM BLAKE

Upon a Snail

She goes but softly, but she goeth sure,
    She stumbles not, as stronger creatures do;
Her journey's shorter, so she may endure
    Better than they which do much further go.

She makes no noise, but stilly seizeth on
    The flower or herb appointed for her food;
The which she quietly doth feed upon,
    While others range, and glare, but find no good.

And though she doth but very softly go,
    However slow her pace be, yet 'tis sure;
And certainly they that do travel so,
    The prize which they do aim at, they procure.

JOHN BUNYAN

Upon a Spider Catching a Fly

Thou sorrow, venom elf:
    Is this thy play,
To spin a web out of thyself
    To catch a fly?
        For why?

I saw a pettish wasp
    Fall foul therein,
Whom yet thy whorl-pins did not clasp
    Lest he should fling
        His sting.

But as afraid, remote
    Didst stand hereat
And with thy little fingers stroke
    And gently tap
        His back.

Thus gently him didst treat

Lest he should pet,
And in a froppish, waspish heat
    Should greatly fret
        Thy net.

Whereas the silly fly,
    Caught by its leg
Thou by the throat tookst hastily
    And hind the head
        Bite dead.

This goes to pot, that not
    Nature doth call.
Strive not above what strength hath got
    Lest in the brawl
        Thou fall.

This fray seems thus to us.
    Hell's spider gets
His entrails spun to whip-cords thus,
    And wove to nets
        And sets.

To tangle Adam's race
    In's strategems
To their destructions, spoiled, made base
    By venom things,
        Damned sins.

But mighty, gracious Lord
    Communicate
Thy grace to break the cord, afford
    Us glory's gate
        And state.

We'll nightingale sing like
    When perched on high
In glory's cage, thy glory, bright,
    And thankfully,
        For joy.

EDWARD TAYLOR

The Victor Dog

For Elizabeth Bishop

Bix to Buxtehude to Boulez,
The little white dog on the Victor label
Listens long and hard as he is able.
It's all in a day's work, whatever plays.

From judgment, it would seem, he has refrained.
He even listens earnestly to Bloch,
Then builds a church upon our acid rock.
He's man's – no – he's the Leiermann's best friend,

Or would be if hearing and listening were the same.
Does he hear? I fancy he rather smells
Those lemon-gold arpeggios in Ravel's
'Les jets d'eau du palais de ceux qui s'aiment.'

He ponders the Schumann Concerto's tall willow hit
By lightning, and stays put. When he surmises
Through one of Bach's eternal boxwood mazes
The oboe pungent as a bitch in heat,

Or when the calypso decants its raw bay rum
Or the moon in *Wozzeck* reddens ripe for murder,
He doesn't sneeze or howl; just listens harder.
Adamant needles bear down on him from

Whirling of outer space, too black, too near –
But he was taught as a puppy not to flinch,
Much less to imitate his bête noire Blanche
Who barked, fat foolish creature, at King Lear.

Still others fought in the road's filth over Jezebel,
Slavered on hearths of horned and pelted barons.
His forebears lacked, to say the least, forbearance.
Can nature change in him? Nothing's impossible.

The last chord fades. The night is cold and fine.
His master's voice rasps through the grooves' bare groves.
Obediently, in silence like the grave's
He sleeps there on the still-warm gramophone

Only to dream he is at the première of a Handel
Opera long thought lost – *Il Cane Minore.*
Its allegorical subject is his story!
A little dog revolving round a spindle

Gives rise to harmonies beyond belief,
A cast of stars . . . Is there in Victor's heart
No honey for the vanquished? Art is art.
The life it asks of us is a dog's life.

JAMES MERRILL

View of a Pig

The pig lay on a barrow dead.
It weighed, they said, as much as three men.
Its eyes closed, pink white eyelashes.
Its trotters stuck straight out.

Such weight and thick pink bulk
Set in death seemed not just dead.
It was less than lifeless, further off.
It was like a sack of wheat.

I thumped it without feeling remorse.
One feels guilty insulting the dead,
Walking on graves. But this pig
Did not seem able to accuse.

It was too dead. Just so much
A poundage of lard and pork.
Its last dignity had entirely gone.
It was not a figure of fun.

Too dead now to pity.
To remember its life, din, stronghold
Of earthly pleasure as it had been,
Seemed a false effort, and off the point.

Too deadly factual. Its weight
Oppressed me – how could it be moved?
And the trouble of cutting it up!
The gash in its throat was shocking, but not pathetic.

Once I ran at a fair in the noise
To catch a greased piglet
That was faster and nimbler than a cat,
Its squeal was the rending of metal.

Pigs must have hot blood, they feel like ovens.
Their bite is worse than a horse's –
They chop a half-moon clean out.
They eat cinders, dead cats.

Distinctions and admirations such
As this one was long finished with.
I stared at it a long time. They were going to scald it,
Scald it and scour it like a doorstep.

TED HUGHES

The Vulture

The Vulture eats between his meals
    And that's the reason why
He very, very rarely feels
    As well as you and I.

His eye is dull, his head is bald,
    His neck is growing thinner.
Oh! what a lesson for us all
    To only eat at dinner!

HILAIRE BELLOC

Wagtail and Baby

A baby watched a ford, whereto
    A wagtail came for drinking;
A blaring bull went wading through,
    The wagtail showed no shrinking.

A stallion splashed his way across,
    The birdie nearly sinking;
He gave his plumes a twitch and toss,
    And held his own unblinking.

Next saw the baby round the spot
    A mongrel slowly slinking:
The wagtail gazed, but faltered not
    In dip and sip and prinking.

A perfect gentleman then neared;
    The wagtail, in a winking,
With terror rose and disappeared;
    The baby fell a-thinking.

    THOMAS HARDY

from Waiting for Godot

VLADIMIR:
A dog came in the kitchen
And stole a crust of bread.
The cook up with a ladle
And beat him till he was dead.

Then all the dogs came running
And dug the dog a tomb –
    [*He stops, broods, resumes.*]

Then all the dogs came running
And dug the dog a tomb
And wrote upon the tombstone
For the eyes of dogs to come:

A dog came in the kitchen
And stole a crust of bread.
Then cook up with a ladle
And beat him till he was dead.

Then all the dogs came running
And dug the dog a tomb –
  [*He stops. As before.*]

Then all the dogs came running
And dug the dog a tomb –
  [*He stops. As before. Softly.*]

And dug the dog a tomb . . .

  SAMUEL BECKETT

The Whale

Now will I in another song make known,
Reveal in words, with verse-craft, from my mind
About a race of fish, the mighty whale.
He often is found fierce and grim of heart,
Not by their wish, to travellers by sea,
To every man; this sailor of the sea-streams
Has got the name of Fastitocolon.
His countenance is like the rugged stone
As if the greatest mass of sea-weed lay
Beside the shore, with sand-banks all around,
So that the seafarers are made to think
That they look on some island with their eyes;
And then they fasten up their high-prowed ship
With cables on that land which is no land,
Tie the sea-horses at the water's edge,
And so onto the island up they go
In cheerful spirits, while their vessels stand
Fast by the shore, encircled by the currents.
Then weary-spirited the voyagers
Set up their camp, they have no thought of danger,

And on that island they start kindling flames,
Make a great fire; the heroes are in joy,
Though tired in spirit, longing for their rest.
Then, skilled in evil-doing, he perceives
The travellers are firmly settled on him,
Live in their camp delighting in good weather,
And suddenly into the salt sea wave
The creature of the ocean sinks with them
Rapidly downwards, visits the sea-bed,
And in that hall of death sets ships and men
To drown. Such is the practice of the demons,
The way of devils, that by acting thus
By secret power they deceive the troop,
By fraud persuade them to renounce good deeds,
Wilfully tempt them so they sadly seek
Comfort from enemies, till in the end
They firmly choose their home with their betrayer.
When the deceitful wicked fiend perceives
By vivid torment that some humankind,
Some race of men, have firmly fixed themselves
In his dominions, then he makes himself
By cruel craft their slayer afterwards,
Who in their pride and arrogance perform
His will on earth with crime; suddenly then
With helmet on which hides him from men's sight,
Lacking in goodness he goes down to hell,
The baseless surge beneath the misty gloom,
Like the great whale which sinks the voyagers,
Both men and ships. He has another way,
That proud seafarer, yet more marvellous.
When hunger comes upon him in the sea
And the grim creature wishes to have food,
Then the sea-guardian opens up his mouth,
His gaping lips; a pleasant smell comes forth
From his insides, and by it other kinds
Of fishes of the sea become deceived
And, swift in swimming, go where the sweet smell
Emerges from him. Then they pass therein
In an unwary crowd, till the wide jaw
Is altogether filled; then suddenly

He shuts the grisly jaws together round
His booty; so it is for every man,
He who most often thinks about his life
Heedlessly in this transitory time,
Lets himself be deceived by the sweet smell,
The false desire, that he is stained by sin
Against the King of Glory. The accursed
Opens hell's gates after their going hence
For those who foolish gave themselves in sin
To fleshly joys rather than what is right.
When the malicious one, skilful in sin,
Has brought in those who used to call on him
To that safe place, that whirlpool of hot fire,
Loaded with guilt, and those who formerly
Keenly obeyed his orders in their lives,
Then he snaps shut the grisly jaws on them,
Firmly together the strong doors of hell
After their death; and those who come therein
Have no return, escape, or parting ever,
Just as the fish who swim upon the sea
Can never turn away from the whale's grasp.

... The Lord of Lords, and ever fight the devil
With words and deeds, that we may see the King
Of Glory. Let us ever seek from Him
Peace and salvation in this passing time,
That we with Him so dear may live in bliss,
May dwell in glory to eternity.

ANONYMOUS
Translated from the Old English by Richard Hamer

'Where the bee sucks, there suck I'

Where the bee sucks, there suck I:
In a cowslip's bell I lie;
There I couch when owls do cry.
On the bat's back I do fly

After summer merrily.
Merrily, merrily shall I live now
Under the blossom that hangs on the bough.

WILLIAM SHAKESPEARE

from The White Devil

Call for the robin-redbreast and the wren,
Since o'er shady groves they hover
And with leaves and flowers do cover
The friendless bodies of unburied men.
Call unto his funeral dole
The ant, the field-mouse, and the mole,
To rear him hillocks that shall keep him warm
And, when gay tombs are robbed, sustain no harm;
But keep the wolf far thence, that's foe to men,
For with his nails he'll dig them up again.

JOHN WEBSTER

The White-Tailed Hornet

The white-tailed hornet lives in a balloon
That floats against the ceiling of the woodshed.
The exit he comes out at like a bullet
Is like the pupil of a pointed gun.
And having power to change his aim in flight,
He comes out more unerring than a bullet.
Verse could be written on the certainty
With which he penetrates my best defense
Of whirling hands and arms about the head
To stab me in the sneeze-nerve of a nostril.
Such is the instinct of it I allow.
Yet how about the insect certainty
That in the neighborhood of home and children

Is such an execrable judge of motives
As not to recognize in me the exception
I like to think I am in everything –
One who would never hang above a bookcase
His Japanese crepe-paper globe for trophy?
He stung me first and stung me afterward.
He rolled me off the field head over heels
And would not listen to my explanations.

That's when I went as visitor to his house.
As visitor at my house he is better.
Hawking for flies about the kitchen door,
In at one door perhaps and out another,
Trust him then not to put you in the wrong.
He won't misunderstand your freest movements.
Let him light on your skin unless you mind
So many prickly grappling feet at once.
He's after the domesticated fly
To feed his thumping grubs as big as he is.
Here he is at his best, but even here –
I watched him where he swooped, he pounced, he struck;
But what he found he had was just a nailhead.
He struck a second time. Another nailhead.
'Those are just nailheads. Those are fastened down.'
Then disconcerted and not unannoyed,
He stooped and struck a little huckleberry
The way a player curls around a football.
'Wrong shape, wrong color, and wrong scent,' I said.
The huckleberry rolled him on his head.
At last it was a fly. He shot and missed;
And the fly circled round him in derision.
But for the fly he might have made me think
He had been at his poetry, comparing
Nailhead with fly and fly with huckleberry:
How like a fly, how very like a fly.
But the real fly he missed would never do;
The missed fly made me dangerously skeptic.

Won't this whole instinct matter bear revision?
Won't almost any theory bear revision?
To err is human, not to, animal.

Or so we pay the compliment to instinct,
Only too liberal of our compliment
That really takes away instead of gives.
Our worship, humor, conscientiousness
Went long since to the dogs under the table.
And served us right for having instituted
Downward comparisons. As long on earth
As our comparisons were stoutly upward
With gods and angels, we were men at least,
But little lower than the gods and angels.
But once comparisons were yielded downward,
Once we began to see our images
Reflected in the mud and even dust,
'Twas disillusion upon disillusion.
We were lost piecemeal to the animals,
Like people thrown out to delay the wolves.
Nothing but fallibility was left us;
And this day's work made even that seem doubtful.

ROBERT FROST

'Who so list to hount, I knowe where is an hynde'

Who so list to hount, I knowe where is an hynde,
   But as for me, helas, I may no more:
   The vayne travaill hath weried me so sore.
   I ame of theim that farthest commeth behinde;
Yet may I by no meanes my weried mynde
   Drawe from the Diere: but as she fleeth afore,
Faynting I folowe. I leve of therefore,
   Sins in a nett I seke to hold the wynde.
Who list her hount, I put him owte of dowbte,
   As well as I may spend his tyme in vain:
   And, graven with Diamonds, in letters plain

There is written her faier neck rounde abowte:
   Noli me tangere, for Cesars I ame;
   And wylde for to hold, though I seme tame.

THOMAS WYATT

Widgeon

For Paul Muldoon

It had been badly shot.
While he was plucking it
he found, he says, the voice box –

like a flute stop
in the broken windpipe –

and blew upon it
unexpectedly
his own small widgeon cries.

SEAMUS HEANEY

The Wild Swans at Coole

The trees are in their autumn beauty,
The woodland paths are dry,
Under the October twilight the water
Mirrors a still sky;
Upon the brimming water among the stones
Are nine-and-fifty swans.

The nineteenth autumn has come upon me
Since I first made my count;
I saw, before I had well finished,
All suddenly mount
And scatter wheeling in great broken rings
Upon their clamorous wings.

I have looked upon those brilliant creatures,
And now my heart is sore.
All's changed since I, hearing at twilight,
The first time on this shore,
The bell-beat of their wings above my head,
Trod with a lighter tread.

Unwearied still, lover by lover,
They paddle in the cold
Companionable streams or climb the air;
Their hearts have not grown old;
Passion or conquest, wander where they will,
Attend upon them still.

But now they drift on the still water,
Mysterious, beautiful;
Among what rushes will they build,
By what lake's edge or pool
Delight men's eyes when I awake some day
To find they have flown away?

W. B. YEATS

The Windhover

To Christ our Lord

I caught this morning morning's minion, king-
   dom of daylight's dauphin, dapple-dawn-drawn Falcon, in his riding
  Of the rolling level underneath him steady air, and striding
High there, how he rung upon the rein of a wimpling wing
In his ecstasy! then off, off forth on swing,
   As a skate's heel sweeps smooth on a bow-bend: the hurl and gliding
  Rebuffed the big wind. My heart in hiding
Stirred for a bird, – the achieve of, the mastery of the thing!

Brute beauty and valour and act, oh, air, pride, plume, here
  Buckle! AND the fire that breaks from thee then, a billion
Times told lovelier, more dangerous, O my chevalier!

No wonder of it: shéer plód makes plough down sillion
Shine, and blue-bleak embers, ah my dear,
    Fall, gall themselves, and gash gold-vermilion.

GERARD MANLEY HOPKINS

Wodwo

What am I? Nosing here, turning leaves over
Following a faint stain on the air to the river's edge
I enter water. What am I to split
The glassy grain of water looking upward I see the bed
Of the river above me upside down very clear
What am I doing here in mid-air? Why do I find
this frog so interesting as I inspect its most secret
interior and make it my own? Do these weeds
know me and name me to each other have they
seen me before, do I fit in their world? I seem
separate from the ground and not rooted but dropped
out of nothing casually I've no threads
fastening me to anything I can go anywhere
I seem to have been given the freedom
of this place what am I then? And picking
bits of bark off this rotten stump gives me
no pleasure and it's no use so why do I do it
me and doing that have coincided very queerly
But what shall I be called am I the first
have I an owner what shape am I what
shape am I am I huge if I go
to the end on this way past these trees and past these trees
till I get tired that's touching one wall of me
for the moment if I sit still how everything
stops to watch me I suppose I am the exact centre
but there's all this what is it roots
roots roots roots and here's the water
again very queer but I'll go on looking

TED HUGHES

Yoko

All today I lie in the bottom of the wardrobe
feeling low but sometimes getting up
to moodily lumber across rooms
and lap from the toilet bowl, it is so sultry
and then I hear the noise of firecrackers again
all New York is jaggedy with firecrackers today
and I go back to the wardrobe gloomy
trying to void my mind of them.
I am confused, I feel loose and unfitted.

At last deep in the stairwell I hear a tread,
it is him, my leader, my love.
I run to the door and listen to his approach.
Now I can smell him, what a good man he is,
I love it when he has the sweat of work on him,
as he enters I yodel with happiness,
I throw my body up against his, I try to lick his lips,
I care about him more than anything.

After we eat we go for a walk to the piers.
I leap into the standing warmth, I plunge into
the combination of old and new smells.
Here on a garbage can at the bottom, so interesting,
what sister or brother I wonder left this message I sniff.
I too piss there, and go on.
Here a hydrant there a pole
here's a smell I left yesterday, well that's disappointing
but I piss there anyway, and go on.

I investigate so much that in the end
it is for form's sake only, only a drop comes out.

I investigate tar and rotten sandwiches, everything, and go on.

And here a dried old turd, so interesting
so old, so dry, yet so subtle and mellow.
I can place it finely, I really appreciate it,
a gold distant smell like packed autumn leaves in winter
reminding me how what is rich and fierce when excreted

becomes weathered and mild
                              but always interesting
and reminding me of what I have to do.

My leader looks on and expresses his approval.

I sniff it well and later I sniff the air well
a wind is meeting us after the close July day
rain is getting near too but first the wind.

Joy, joy,
being outside with you, active, investigating it all,
with bowels emptied, feeling your approval
and then running on, the big fleet Yoko,
my body in its excellent black coat never lets me down,
returning to you (as I always will, you know that)
and now
              filling myself out with myself, no longer confused,
my panting pushing apart my black lips, but unmoving,
I stand with you braced against the wind.

THOM GUNN

The Zebras

To Chips Rafferty

From the dark woods that breathe of fallen showers,
Harnessed with level rays in golden reins,
The zebras draw the dawn across the plains
Wading knee-keep among the scarlet flowers.
The sunlight, zithering their flanks with fire,
Flashes between the shadows as they pass
Barred with electric tremors through the grass
Like wind along the gold strings of a lyre.

Into the flushed air snorting rosy plumes
That smoulder round their feet in drifting fumes,
With dove-like voices call the distant fillies,

While round the herds the stallion wheels his flight,
Engine of beauty volted with delight,
To roll his mare among the trampled lilies.

ROY CAMPBELL

Acknowledgements

The editor and publishers gratefully acknowledge permission to reprint copyright material in this book as follows:

HANS ARP: Georges Borchardt Inc. for 'I am a horse', translated by Michael Benedikt from *The Poetry of Surrealism* (Little, Brown & Company). JOHN ASHBERY: Carcanet Press Ltd for 'Glazunoviana' from *Selected Poems* (1986). W. H. AUDEN: Faber & Faber Ltd. for 'Hunting Season', 'The Fall of Rome' and 'Address to the Beasts' from *Collected Poems*. SAMUEL BECKETT: Faber & Faber Ltd for an extract from *Waiting for Godot*. HILAIRE BELLOC: The Peters Fraser & Dunlop Group Ltd on behalf of The Estate of Hilaire Belloc for 'The Vulture' and 'Jim Who ran away from his Nurse, and was eaten by a Lion' from *Cautionary Verses* (Random House UK Ltd). ELIZABETH BISHOP: Farrar, Straus & Giroux Inc. for 'The Armadillo', 'The Fish', 'The Man-Moth' and 'The Moose' from *The Complete Poems 1927–1979*, copyright © 1979, 1983 by Alice Helen Methfessel. ROY CAMPBELL: Francisco Campbell Custodio and Ad Donker Publishers for 'The Zebras' from *The Selected Poems of Roy Campbell*, chosen by Peter Alexander (Oxford University Press, 1982). CIARAN CARSON: the author and The Gallery Press for 'The Albatross' from *First Language* (1993). G. K. CHESTERTON: A. P. Watt Ltd. on behalf of The Royal Literary Fund for 'The Donkey' from *Collected Poems*. HART CRANE: Liveright Publishing Corporation for 'A Name for All' from *Complete Poems of Hart Crane*, edited by Marc Simon, copyright 1933, copyright © 1958, 1966 by Liveright Publishing Corporation, copyright © 1986 by Marc Simon. KEVIN CROSSLEY-HOLLAND: the author c/o Rogers, Coleridge & White Ltd., 20 Powis Mews, London W11 1JN, for his translations from *The Exeter Book of Riddles* (Penguin Books, 1979), copyright © 1993 Kevin Crossley-Holland. E. E. CUMMINGS: W. W. Norton & Company Ltd. for 't,h;r:u;s,h;e:s' from *Complete Poems 1904–1962*, edited by George J. Firmage, copyright © 1991 by the Trustees for the E. E. Cummings Trust and George James Firmage. JAMES DICKEY: University Press of New England for 'The Heaven of Animals' from *Collected Poems 1957–1967*, copyright © 1967 by Wesleyan University Press. EMILY DICKINSON: Harvard University Press and the Trustees of Amherst College for 'A Bird came down the Walk' (No. 328), 'His Mansion in the Pool' (No. 1379), 'I heard a Fly buzz – when I died' (No. 465), 'A narrow Fellow in the Grass' (No. 986) and 'Our little Kinsmen – after Rain' (No. 885) from *The Poems of Emily Dickinson*, edited by Thomas H. Johnson, Cambridge, Massachusetts: The Belknap Press of Harvard University Press, copyright © 1951, 1955, 1979, 1983 by the President and Fellows of Harvard College. RICHARD EBERHART: Oxford University Press Inc. for 'The

author and The Gallery Press for 'The Trout' from *Collected Poems* (1995).
MARIANNE MOORE: Faber & Faber Ltd for 'To a Snail', 'A Jelly-Fish', 'The
Fish' and 'Elephants' from *The Complete Poems*. EDWIN MUIR: Faber &
Faber Ltd for 'The Horses' from *Collected Poems*. LES MURRAY: Carcanet Press
Ltd, Margaret Connolly & Associates Pty Ltd. and Farrar, Straus & Giroux
Inc. for 'Goose to Donkey', 'Pigs' and 'Two Dogs' from *Translations from the
Natural World* (1993). TOM PAULIN: Faber & Faber Ltd, for 'A Rum Cove,
a Stout Cove' from *Liberty Tree*. ROBERT PINSKY: Farrar, Straus & Giroux Inc.
and Carcanet Press Ltd for Canto I from *The Inferno of Dante: A New Verse
Translation*, copyright © 1994 by Farrar, Straus & Giroux Inc., translation
copyright © 1994 by Robert Pinsky. SYLVIA PLATH: Faber & Faber Ltd for
'Ariel', 'Blue Moles' and 'The Swarm' from *Collected Poems*. FRANCIS PONGE:
Wake Forest University Press for 'The Horse', translated by John Montague,
from *Selected Poems*. CRAIG RAINE: Oxford University Press for 'Pretty Baa
Lamb' from *A Martian Sends a Postcard Home*, copyright © Craig Raine,
1993. CHRISTOPHER REID: Faber & Faber Ltd for 'Two Dogs on a Pub Roof'
from *Expanded Universes*. ADRIENNE RICH: the author and W. W. Norton &
Company Inc. for 'Abnegation' from *Collected Early Poems: 1950–1970*,
copyright © 1969 by W. W. Norton & Company. THEODORE ROETHKE:
Faber & Faber Ltd for 'The Sloth' from *The Collected Poems of Theodore
Roethke*. DELMORE SCHWARTZ: New Directions Publishing Corporation and
Laurence Pollinger Ltd for 'The Heavy Bear Who Goes With Me' from *Selected
Poems: Summer Knowledge*, copyright © 1959 by Delmore Schwartz. JAMES
STEPHENS: The Society of Authors as the Literary Representative of the Estate
of James Stephens for 'The Snare' from *Collected Poems* (Macmillan).
WALLACE STEVENS: Faber & Faber Ltd and Alfred A. Knopf Inc. for 'Thirteen
Ways of Looking at a Blackbird' and 'A Rabbit as King of the Ghosts' from
The Collected Poems of Wallace Stevens. RICHARD WILBUR: Harcourt Brace &
Company for 'The Death of a Toad' from *Ceremony and Other Poems*, copyright
1950 and renewed 1978 by Richard Wilbur, and 'A Black November Turkey'
from *Things of This World*, copyright 1953 and renewed 1981 by Richard
Wilbur; Harcourt Brace & Company and Faber & Faber Ltd for 'The Ride'
and 'Jean De La Fontaine: The Grasshopper and the Ant' from *New and
Collected Poems*, copyright © 1982 by Richard Wilbur. C. K. WILLIAMS: Farrar,
Straus & Giroux Inc. and Richard Scott Simon Ltd. for 'The Dog' from
Poems 1963–1983, copyright © 1988 by C. K. Williams. WILLIAM CARLOS
WILLIAMS: Carcanet Press Ltd and New Directions Publishing Corporation
for 'The Horse' from *Collected Poems 1909–1939*, Volume 1, copyright ©
1938 by New Directions Publishing Corporation, and 'The Polar Bear' from
Collected Poems 1939–1962, Volume 2, copyright © 1962 by William Carlos
Williams. JAMES WRIGHT: University Press of New England for 'Lying in a
Hammock at William Duffy's Home in Pine Island, Minnesota' and 'A Blessing'
from *Above the River: The Complete Poems* (Wesleyan University Press).

Index